Questions and Answers in Agricultural Sciences

Questions and Answers in Agricultural Sciences

Rupinder Singh
ICAR-NET, Gold Medallist
Department of Agriculture
Government of Jammu & Kashmir

A Paperback Division of

NEW INDIA PUBLISHING AGENCY

101, Vikas Surya Plaza, CU Block, LSC Market
Pitam Pura, New Delhi 110 034, India
Phone: + 91 (11)27 34 17 17 Fax: + 91(11) 27 34 16 16
Email: info@nipabooks.com
Web: www.nipabooks.com

Feedback at feedbacks@nipabooks.com

ISBN: 978-93-85516-99-3

Composed, Designed and Printed in India

Dedicated to
NATURE

Preface

This book is mainly written to update the students regarding the latest trend in agriculture competitive examinations.

Presently there is no agriculture objective book which provides platform to students who are preparing for State Public Service Commission Exams. A sincere and hardworking effort has been made to equip them with the latest trend and to upgrade them with the pattern and style of questions generally asked in such examinations. This book would definitely help students to evaluate and asses themselves and check their loopholes.

This book contains eight solved papers of PSC of four States and also includes FAQs covering eight discipline of agriculture. I hope this book would serve the need of the readers and would encourage more and more candidates to opt agriculture in their prelims and would be beneficial to most of the candidates who are preparing for competitive examination in agriculture as optional subject.

Constructive suggestions of students preparing for competitive exams are invited for further improvement of this book.

I express my heartfelt gratitude to my wife Mrs. Gunish Kour and my son Binwant Singh for providing their whole hearted cooperation and support during the write up of this book.

Rupinder Singh

ICAR-NET, Gold Medallist

Contents

Preface .... *vii*

Screening Test-2014 Assistant Floriculture Officer 1

Combined Competitive (Preliminary) Examination, 2013 15

Combined Competitive (Preliminary) Examination, 2012 29

Combined Competitive (Preliminary) Examination, 2011 43

Combined Competitive (Preliminary) Examination, 2010 55

State Public Service Commission (Raao, Agriculture Assistant Officer-2013) 69

State Public Service Commission (HCSEX Agriculture Prelims-2014) 83

State Public Service Commission (Manipur AAO-2015) 95

Selective Questions (FAQ) 111

Selective Questions of Horticulture 119

Selective Questions of Plant Pathology 129

Selective Questions of Entomology 135

Selective Questions of Agriculture Extension 139

Selective Questions of Plant Physiology 147

Selective Questions of Genetics and Plant Breeding 153

Selective Questions of Soil Science 163

Selective Questions of Agronomy 171

Screening Test-2014 Assistant Floriculture Officer

1. The Rashtriya Krishi Vikas Yojana was launched on

   (a) 16th Aug 2004 (b) 15th Aug 2006

   (c) 16th Aug 2007 (d) 15th Aug 2009

2. Per capita arable area is highest in

   (a) Australia (b) Japan

   (c) Canada (d) India

3. Nitrogenous fertilizer with highest nitrogen content

   (a) Urea (b) Anhydrous ammonia

   (c) Ammonium Chloride (d) None

4. Greening in potato is due to

   (a) High temperature (b) High light intensity

   (c) Low temperature (d) All

5. Acricity in colocasia is due to

   (a) Calcium oxalates (b) Potassium

   (c) Sulphur (d) Molybednum

6. Yellow Revolution is also called as oilseed technology mission was launched during the Prime-ministership of

   (a) Indira Gandhi (b) Rajiv Gandhi

   (c) P.V. Narshimha Rao (d) A.B. Vajpayee

7. Moon series of GM Crop related to

   (a) Carnation (b) Rose

   (c) Petunia (d) Chrysanthemum

8. Which annual is of Indian Origin?

   (a) Balsam (b) Zinnia

   (c) Phlox (d) None

9. Xeriscaping includes
   (a) Landscaping in arid areas (b) Use of xerophytic plants for indoor decoration
   (c) Soil conservation measures (d) All

Answers 1 (c) 2 (a) 3 (b) 4 (b) 5 (a) 6 (b) 7 (a) 8 (a) 9 (d)

10. In mustard which type of incompatibility exists?
   (a) Sporophytic (b) Gametophytic
   (c) Both (d) None

11. Inhibition of ethylene biosynthesis can be achieved by suppression of expression of
   (a) ACC oxidase (b) ACC synthase
   (c) Both I and II (d) None

12. Aristolochia represents a group of
   (a) Deciduous woody vine (b) Herbaceous perennials
   (c) Climber (d) All

13. Phototphosphorylation is
   (a) Hill reaction (b) Formation of ATP in presence of light
   (c) Formation of NADP in presence of light (d) None

14. Largest genera of orchid is
   (a) Dendrobium (b) Bulbophyllum
   (c) Catteleya (d) Cymbidium

15. Terrarium is
   (a) Plant grown on terraces (b) Transparent container having miniature garden developed inside
   (c) Solution used in flowers (d) Pot for raising plants

16. Why is blanching practiced in vegetables?
   (a) Micro organism removal (b) In-activate enzyme
   (c) For softening the vegetables (d) All

17. The term "Heaven on earth" is used for garden
   (a) Japanese garden (b) Mughal garden
   (c) Italian garden (d) Persian garden

18. How much area is required for raising nursery for planting one hectare of rice?

(a) 1/5 of total area (b) 1/10 of total area

(c) 1/15 of total area (d) 1/20 of total area

Answers 10 (a) 11 (c) 12 (d) 13 (b) 14 (a) 15 (b) 16 (d) 17 (b) 18 (b)

19. Which of the following is a food additive?

(a) Antisalting agent (b) Antioxidants

(c) Fat Emulsification (d) All of the above

20. Pigment responsible for orange colour

(a) Pelargonidins (b) Cyanidins

(c) Anthocynin (d) Delphinins

21. Which of following is fire hazardous fertilizer?

(a) Ammonium sulphate (b) Ammonium nitrate

(c) Calcium ammonium nitrate (d) Urea

22. In India which is the second rank pulse crop?

(a) Bengal gram (b) Pigeon pea

(c) Lentil (d) Moong

23. The most processed product from arecanut is

(a) Kottapak (b) Kalipak

(c) Nuli (d) all

24. Which is non bulb forming member of onion family?

(a) Leek (b) Garlic

(c) Onion (d) None

25. Which of following is sympodial orchid?

(a) Vanda (b) Archis

(c) Dendrobium (d) None

26. The term epistasis is given by

(a) Mendel (b) Halman

(c) Bateson (d) Hull

27. Calyx splitting is the major problem in

(a) Orchid (b) Rose

(c) Carnation (d) Marigold

Answers 19 (b) 20 (a) 21 (b) 22 (b) 23 (b) 24 (a) 25 (d) 26 (c) 27 (c)

28. In anthurium which is cut flower spp?
(a) *A. odarum* (b) *A. adreanum*
(c) Both (d) None

29. Correlation coefficient lies between
(a) 0 to 1 (b) 1
(c) 0 (d) -1 to +1

30 The quick freezing is preferred over slow freezing, due to
(a) Formation of small crystal (b) Formation of large crystal
(c) To save time (d) none

31. Which of the following is class one preservative?
(a) Silver nitrate (b) KMS
(c) Sugar (d) Vinegar

32. Which is the 20th Century vegetable?
(a) Cluster bean (b) Amaranthus
(c) Brinjal (d) Winged bean

33. Metaxenia is observed in
(a) Root crops (b) Tuber crops
(c) Bulb crops (d) Cucurbits

34. 'Bahar' is a popular variety of
(a) Pea (b) Groundnut
(c) Pigeonpea (d) Gram

35. 'Pusa Bold' is a variety of
(a) Wheat (b) Mustard
(c) Gram (d) Groundnut

36. Directorate of Floriculture is located in
(a) Delhi (b) Pune
(c) Bangalore (d) Kolkata

Answers 28 (b) 29 (d) 30 (b) 31 (d) 32 (d) 33 (d) 34 (c) 35 (b) 36 (a)

37. Rice Gandhibug is scientifically known as
(a) *Oresalia oryzea* (b) *Leptocorisa acuta*
(c) *Benesia tabacia* (d) None

38. Green manure should be incorporated at its
(a) Seedling stage (b) Fully matured stage
(c) Flowering stage (d) Drying stage

39. The fruit of wheat is known as

(a) Pod (b) Capsule

(c) Siliqua (d) Caryopsis

40. Carnation is national flower of

(a) Japan (b) China

(c) Spain (d) Holland

41. Endosperm is missing in seed of

(a) Carnation (b) Rose

(c) Chrysanthemum (d) Orchid

42. The chemical generally used as germicide in vase solution is

(a) Sucrose (b) HQC

(c) $Ca(Nos)_2$ (d) MH

43. Herkogamy favours

(a) Self pollination (b) Cross pollination

(c) Mutation (d) Wide hybridisation

44. For sugar translocation of grape which of the following elements is necessary?

(a) B (b) Ca

(c) Mg (d) Phosphorous

45. For measuring leaf area following instrument is used

(a) Alanometer (b) Anemometer

(c) Porometer (d) Barometer

Answers 37 (b) 38 (c) 39 (d) 40 (c) 41 (d) 42 (b) 43 (b) 44 (a) 45 (c)

46. Permissible limit of SO_2 in Jam is

(a) 300 ppm (b) 40 ppm

(c) 70 ppm (d) 100 ppm

47. Anther mutant cultivar of tomato is

(a) Pusa Divya (b) Pusa Gaurav

(c) Pusa Ruby (d) None

48. Maturity of pea is measured by

(a) Derometer (b) Refractometer

(c) Alanometer (d) Tendrometer

49. In fruit jelly pectin and sugar is present in ratio of

(a) 1:65 (b) 65:1

(c) 65:33 (d) 33:65

50. Largest genera of orchid is
   (a) Dendrobium (b) Bulbophyllum
   (c) Catteleya (d) Cymbidium

51. For population improvement in any crop, best method is
   (a) Pureline selection (b) Pedigree selection
   (c) Mass selection (d) Recurrent selection

52. Replacement of one pair of chromosome of cultivated spp with those of wild donar spp
   (a) Alien substitution (b) Alien addition
   (c) Introgression (d) Somatic hybridization

53. The most effective method of transfer of oligogene character is
   (a) Pedigree breeding (b) Bulk breeding
   (c) Back cross method (d) None

54. Diploid apogamy is found in
   (a) Allium spp (b) Parthinium spp
   (c) Tobacco (d) Rice

Answers 46 (b) 47 (a) 48 (d) 49 (d) 50 (a)51 (d)52 (a) 53 (c) 54 (a)

55. Which vegetable is dioecious in nature and propagated by stem cutting?
   (a) Spinach (b) Sweet potato
   (c) Tobacco (d) Pointed gourd

56. Yellow colour of onion is due to
   (a) Myrecetin (b) Qucertin
   (c) Allicin (d) Malvelin

57. Wine is preserved at
   (a) 10% alcohol (b) 14% alcohol
   (c) 8% alcohol (d) 5% alcohol

58. A bud mutant cultivar of mango is
   (a) Noorjahan (b) Rosica
   (c) Creton (d) Ratna

59. Sulphur fungicide can be freely used on all vegetables except
   (a) Peas and bean (b) Root vegetables
   (c) Cucurbits (d) Okra

60. If chromosome complement of two diploid spp is combined in one the resultant spp
(a) Monogenic (b) Polygenic
(c) Amphidiploid (d) Haploid

61. In temperate countries sugar is obtained from
(a) Sugarcane (b) Maple
(c) Sugarbeet (d) Wheat

62. Zinc is required for synthesis of
(a) Argenine (b) Proline
(c) Tryptophan (d) Methonin

63. June drop in apple is due to
(a) Lack of pollination (b) Moisture stress
(c) Ca deficiency (d) Alternate bearing

Answers 55 (d) 56 (b) 57 (a) 58 (b) 59 (c) 60 (c) 61 (c) 62 (c) 63 (b)

64. Vegetable containing highest iron content is
(a) Spinach (b) Lettuce
(c) Cabbage (d) Brinjal

65. Gynomonoecious means
(a) All female flower (b) Female and bisexual flowers
(c) Only male flowers (d) Male and female flowers

66. Excessive chloride in tobacco leads to
(a) Bushing of leaves (b) Difacd leaves
(c) Reducing storage life of leaves (d) All

67. Winter banana is variety of
(a) Pear (b) Apple
(c) Papaya (d) Mandarin

68. Which crop grows in high pH soil?
(a) Banana (b) Amla
(c) Papaya (d) Mandarin

69. Which vegetable crop is day neutral?
(a) Tomato (b) Potato
(c) Sweet Potato (d) Spinach

70. Bacterial wilt resistant variety of Tomato is

(a) Arka Abha (b) Arka Vardan
(c) Arka Gaurav (d) All

71. Daily requirement of vegetables is

(a) 150 grams (b) 200 grams
(c) 285 grams (d) 400 grams

72. A chemical extracted form datura which withdraws the reaction of morphine is

(a) Ajmachine (b) Hycosmine
(c) Reserpine (d) Nicotine

Answers 64 (a) 65 (b) 66 (d) 67 (b) 68 (b) 69 (a) 70 (a) 71 (c) 72 (b)

73. ICAR was established on the recommendation of which Commission?

(a) Mehta (b) Lord Linlithgow
(c) B. Vishvanathan (d) None

74. AICRP on floriculture was established in

(a) 1970-71 (b) 1971-72
(c) 1972-73 (d) 1973-74

75. NAARM was established in

(a) 1972 (b) 1976
(c) 1978 (d) 1974

76. *Ikebana originated in*

(a) India (b) Japan
(c) China (d) Korea

77. Genotype of maleness in papaya is

(a) Mm (b) M_2m
(c) mm (d) M_1m

78. In India, the authorative body to approve genetically modified food is

(a) ICAR (b) DBT
(c) GEAC (d) ICGEB

79. NREGA was renamed as MNREGA on

(a) 2nd Oct 2007 (b) 2nd Oct 2008
(c) 2nd Oct 2009 (d) 2nd Oct 2010

80. The Rashtriya Gokul Mission announced by the Union Government aims at
   (a) Protecting the indigenous breeds of cows
   (b) To prevent slaughtering of cattle's
   (c) To increase milk production
   (d) None

81. The planned development model was adopted in India from
   (a) 1st April 1950 (b) 2nd Oct. 1950
   (c) 26th Jan. 1950 (d) 1st May 1950

Answers 73 (b) 74(a) 75 (b) 76 (b) 77 (d) 78 (c)79 (c) 80 (a) 81 (a)

82. Which of the following is a food additive?
   (a) Antisalting agent (b) Antioxidants
   (c) Fat Emulsification (d) All of the above

83. AICRP on floriculture was established in
   (a) 1970-71 (b) 1971-72
   (c) 1972-73 (d) 1973-74

84. Which of the following is not an example of climate catastrophe?
   (a) Drought (b) Flood
   (c) Cyclone (d) Desertification

85. Concrete is
   (a) Non purified form of essential oil
   (b) Concentrated form of essentialoil
   (c) Highly pure form of essential oil
   (d) None

86. Arjun is a mutant cultivar of Bougainvillea, its parent is
   (a) Jaya (b) Shipra
   (c) Partha (d) Ratna

87. The first Sugar Mill in India was set up in 1903 at
   (a) Partapgarh (b) Pratappur
   (c) Mawana (d) Balrampur

88. The leafless variety of pea is
   (a) Arkel (b) Azad Pea-I
   (c) Aparna (d) L-116

89. The pilot project for rural development was started in the year

(a) 1971 (b) 1978
(c) 1952 (d) 1948

90. 'Barani deep' is a variety of

(a) Pea (b) Groundnut
(c) Pigeonpea (d) Gram

Answers 82 (b) 83 (a) 84 (d) 85 (a) 86 (c)87 (b)88 (c) 89 (c) 90 (c)

91. 'Bahar' is a popular variety of

(a) Pea (b) Groundnut
(c) Pigeonpea (d) Gram

92. 'Haryali Yojna' is related to

(a) Soil Management (b) Air Management
(c) Crop Management (d) Water Management

93. India's rank in rice production in the world is

(a) First (b) Second
(c) Third (d) Fourth

94. Balanced Fertilizer Ratio (NPK) for cereal crops is

(a) 1:2:2 (b) 3:2:1
(c) 4:2:1 (d) 2:1:1

95. India's contribution in the world fruit production is

(a) 20% (b) 25%
(c) 10% (d) 15%

96. 'Pusa Bold' is a variety of

(a) Wheat (b) Mustard
(c) Gram (d) Groundnut

97. Which one of the following fruits is most suitable for jelly making?

(a) Mango (b) Papaya
(c) Guava (d) Apple

98. The maximum production of Banana is obtained from the state

(a) Tamil Nadu (b) Maharashtra
(c) Uttar Pradesh (d) Bihar

99. Who among the following has coined the term "Biodiversity" for the first time

(a) C.J. Borrow (b) De Castri

(c) Walter G. Rosen (d) D.R. Batish

Answers 91 (c) 92 (d) 93 (b) 94 (c) 95 (c) 96 (b) 97 (c) 98 (a) 99 (c)

100. 'Pusa 1509' is a new high yielding variety of

(a) Wheat (b) Basmati Rice

(c) Pigeon Pea (d) Mango

101. In fruit jelly pectin and sugar is present in ratio of

(a) 1:65 (b) 65:1

(c) 65:33 (d) 33:65

102. Which hormone is found in gaseous form?

(a) Abscisic Acid (b) Ethylene

(c) Gibberellin (d) Auxin

103. NREGA was renamed as MNREGA on

(a) 2nd Oct 2007 (b) 2nd Oct 2008

(c) 2nd Oct 2009 (d) 2nd Oct 2010

104. Triticale and interspecific hybrid between Wheat and Rye was developed by

(a) Knight (1800) (b) Rimpu (1890)

(c) Davenport (1908) (d) Sewall Wright (1921)

105. First interspecific hybrid was developed by Thomas Fairchild (1717) between

(a) *Tagetus erecta* and *Tegetus patula*

(b) *Dianthus Caryophyllus* and *Dianthus barbatus*

(c) *Chrysanthemum carinatum* and *Chrysanthemum coronarium*

(d) *Chrysanthemum segetum* and *Chrysanthemum carinatum*

106. Knol khol has originated from

(a) *Brassica napus* var. *sylvestris* (b) *Brassica oleracea* var. *napus*

(c) *Brassica oleracea* var. *sylvestris* (d) *Brassica napus* var. *oleracea*

107. When a purine is replaced by anther purine or a pyrimidine is replaced by another pyrimidine it is called as

(a) Substitution (b) Transition

(c) Transversion (d) Deletion

108. Which one of the following is correct in which they appear during biocontrol operations?
   (a) Parasite, Release, Mass rearing, Parasitism
   (b) Mass rearing, Parasite, Release, Parasitism
   (c) Release, Mass rearing, Parasite, Parasitism
   (d) Parasite, Mass rearing, Release, Parasitism

Answers 100 (b) 101(d) 102(b) 103(c) 104(b) 105(b) 106(c) 107(b) 108(d)

109. Arjun is a mutant cultivar of Bougainvillea, its parent is
   (a) Jaya (b) Shipra
   (c) Partha (d) Ratna

110. Betalin imparts
   (a) Pink to red colour (b) Red to Blue colour
   (c) Yellow to orange colour (d) Purple to magenta colour

111. English word *saffron* derived from the word *safranum* is from which language?
   (a) French (b) Latin
   (c) Greek (d) German

112. Saffron is
   (a) Diploid (b) Triploid
   (c) Tetraploid (d) Octaploid

113. Who is DDG horticulture?
   (a) Dr. H. P. Singh (b) Dr. N. K. Krishna Kumar
   (c) Dr. Gorukh Singh (d) Dr. K. L. Chaddha

114. Pulsing is a
   (a) Short term pre-shipment treatment with low concentration of sucrose and with various other chemicals.
   (b) Short term pre-shipment treatment with high concentration of sucrose and with various other chemicals.
   (c) Solution used at pre harvesting stage to enhance shelf life of flowers
   (d) Solution to treat flower to be kept for floral display

115. Which is not an Anti-ethylene compound?
   (a) $AgNO_3$ (b) STS
   (c) 1-MCP (d) 8-HQC

116. Daily requirement of vegetables is
   (a) 150 grams (b) 200 grams
   (c) 285 grams (d) 400 grams

117. Which part of sandalwood is used to extract oil?

(a) Soft wood (b) Hard wood

(c) Heartwood (d) None

Answers: 109 (c) 110 (c) 111 (b) 112 (b) 113 (b) 114 (a) 115 (b) 116 (c) 117 (c)

118. Which is not a bulb?

(a) Tulip (b) Gladiolus

(c) Dassodil (d) Lily

119. A layer of matted earth by grass and plant roots is

(a) Lawn (b) Yard

(c) Turf (d) Garden

120. Which is the largest cut flower producing state of India?

(a) Karnataka (b) Maharashtra

(c) West Bengal (d) Punjab

Answers 118 (b) 119 (c) 120 (c)

Combined Competitive (Preliminary) Examination, 2013

1. The rice varieties grown in India belong to
   (a) Indica (b) Japonica
   (c) Javanica (d) Asiatica
2. The rice inflorescence is known as
   (a) Panicle (b) Spikelet
   (c) Ear (d) Siliqua
3. For transplanting one hectare area of rice how much area is sufficient for nursery raising?
   (a) $100m^2$ (b) $500m^2$
   (c) $1000m^2$ (d) $1500m^2$
4. Tungro virus of rice is transmitted by
   (a) Stem borer (b) Green leaf hopper
   (c) Leaf roller (d) White fly
5. Dwarf wheat (Mexican) is introduced in India by
   (a) Dr. N.E. Borlaug (b) Dr. M.S. Swaminathan
   (c) Dr. B.P. Pal (d) Dr. C. Subramaniam
6. The normal seed rate of wheat is
   (a) 50 kg/ha (b) 75 kg/ha
   (c) 100 kg/ha (d) 125 kg/ha
7. Triticale is a cross between
   (a) Wheat × oat (b) Wheat × barley
   (c) Oat × barley (d) Wheat × Rye
8. Cytoplasmic male sterility is used in
   (a) Hybrid seed production (b) Composite seed production
   (c) Varietal development (d) Biotechnology

9. Most serious disease of Sugarcane is

(a) Red stripe (b) Wilt
(c) Red rot (d) Smut

Answers 1 (a) 2 (a) 3 (c) 4 (b) 5 (a) 6 (c) 7 (d) 8 (a) 9 (c)

10. How many setts are required to plant one hectare of sugarcane?

(a) 30,000-35000 (b) 35,000-40,000
(c) 40,000-45,000 (d) 50,000-55,000

11. In which of the following crops azolla is used as bio-fertilizer?

(a) Rice (b) Sorghum
(c) Sunflower (d) Maize

12. Which of the following crop rotation is the best for maintaining soil fertility?

(a) Maize-toria-wheat (b) Paddy-wheat-maize
(c) Paddy-potato-greengram (d) Soyabean-wheat-greengram

13. The capacity of soil to resist appreciable change in pH value is called

(a) CEC (b) Buffering capacity
(c) Percentage base saturation (d) Anion-exchange capacity

14. Humic acid is a fraction of humus, which is

(a) Soluble in alkali and acid
(b) Insoluble in alkali and soluble in acid
(c) Soluble in alkali and insoluble in acid
(d) Insoluble in both

15. Tetrazolium test is used to determine

(a) Seed purity (b) Seed viability
(c) Seed germination (d) Seed quality

16. Potato is

(a) Modified stem (b) Modified root
(c) Modified leaf (d) Modified flower

17. The type of germination in mungbean is known as

(a) Epigeal (b) Hypogeal
(c) Hypoepigeal (d) Epihypogeal

18. The term "Evergreen Revolution" has been given by

(a) Dr. A.S. Paroda (b) Dr. M.S. Swaminathan
(c) Dr. V.L. Chopra (d) Dr. M.V Rao

Answers 10 (b) 11 (a) 12 (d) 13 (b) 14 (c) 15 (b) 16 (a) 17 (a) 18 (b)

19. Which one of the following microbial agents is being commercially exploited as bio-control agent?
(a) *Penicillium notatum* (b) *Bacillus subtilis*
(c) *Trichoderma viride* (d) *Sclerotium rolfsii*

20. The place of origin of Potato is
(a) China (b) Africa
(c) India (d) South America

21. Excess uptake of which element is known as Luxury consumption?
(a) N (b) P
(c) K (d) Zn

22. Phosphate containing mineral is
(a) Dolomite (b) Apatite
(c) Marble (d) Pyrites

23. Black cotton soil is rich in
(a) Montmorillonite (b) Kaolinite
(c) Illite (d) Chlorite

24. Which form of nitrogen is absorbed by paddy under water logged conditions?
(a) N_2 (b) NH_4 ion
(c) NO_2 ion (d) Nitrate ion

25. Which soil has the highest cation exchange capacity?
(a) Loam (b) Loamy Sand
(c) Sandy Loam (d) Clay Loam

26. Which one of the following causes pungency of mustard oil?
(a) Phenols (b) Amino acids
(c) Glucosinolates (d) Erucic acid

27. Texture of the soil can be changed by
(a) Use of fertilizers (b) Use of tillage practices
(c) Use of manures (d) None of these

Answers 19 (c) 20 (d) 21 (c) 22 (b) 23 (a) 24 (b)25 (d) 26 (c) 27 (d)

28. Khaira disease in rice is caused due to
(a) Fungal infection (b) Bacterial infection
(c) Zinc deficiency (d) Boron deficiency

29. Which one of the following crops has the highest consumption of pesticides?
(a) Cotton (b) Paddy
(c) Oil seeds (d) Pulses

30. Rancidity in Sunflower oil is caused by
(a) Reduction (b) Oxidation
(c) Esterification (d) Nitrification

31. Arkel, Bonneville and Early December are the improved varieties of
(a) Lentil (b) Pea
(c) Gram (d) Safflower

32. Weight of one cotton bale is equal to
(a) 160 Kg (b) 170 Kg
(c) 178 Kg (d) 190 Kg

33. Berseem a fodder crop was introduced in India during 1904 from which country?
(a) South Africa (b) England
(c) Egypt (d) USA

34. The ideal temperature for tuberization in potato is
(a) 14^{0}C (b) 18^{0}C
(c) 21^{0}C (d) 34^{0}C

35. Generally soil pH increases during
(a) Summer (b) Zaid
(c) Winter (d) Post monsoon season

36. Which one of the following elements is considered to be an immobile element in the plants?
(a) Ca (b) Mg
(c) N (d) P

Answers 28 (c) 29 (a) 30 (b) 31 (b) 32 (b) 33 (c) 34 (c) 35 (c) 36 (a)

37. 'P' content in DAP fertilizer is
(a) 20% (b) 36%
(c) 46% (d) 50%

38. Which of the following soils have poor physical condition?
(a) Saline (b) Saline-alkali
(c) Sodic (d) None

39. Vertical section of a soil is known as
(a) Horizones (b) Solum
(c) A soil (d) Profile

40. Which country has largest deposits of 'K'?
(a) India (b) USA
(c) China (d) Canada

41. 'Pungency' in chilli is due to presence of
(a) Amides (b) Sulphur
(c) Capsaicin (d) Boron

42. 'Prabhani Kranti' is a popular variety of
(a) Brinjal (b) Potato
(c) Chilli (d) Okra

43. Gladiolus is propagated by which method?
(a) True seed (b) Bulbs
(c) Stem cutting (d) Roots

44. Which one is a stem vegetable?
(a) Carrot (b) Sweet potato
(c) Radish (d) Knol-khol

45. Yellow coloured fruits and vegetables are rich source of
(a) Vitamin E (b) Vitamin A
(c) Vitamin C (d) Vitamin B

Answers 37 (c) 38 (c) 39 (d) 40 (d)41 (c) 42 (d) 43 (b) 44 (d) 45 (b)

46. Vegetables are canned in
(a) Brine (b) Distilled water
(c) Syrup (d) None of these

47. Wind breaks are planted in Orchards towards
(a) East-South (b) North-West
(c) North-East (d) South-West

48. National Horticulture Board was established in
(a) 1976 (b) 1987
(c) 1984 (d) 1986

49. 'Santa rosa' is a popular variety of
(a) Plum (b) Pear
(c) Cashew nut (d) Walnut

50. Most common training system of apple in India is

(a) Open system (b) Modified leader

(c) Spindle bush system (d) Leader

51. Dwarfing Root stock in mango is

(a) Totapuri Red Small (b) Dashehari

(c) Alphonso (d) Olour

52. Best time for propagation of apple is

(a) Dec.-Jan. (b) Feb.-March

(c) July-Aug. (d) April-May

53. Litchi is commercially propagated by

(a) Veneer grafting (b) Tip layering

(c) Air layering (d) March grafting

54. Which one of the following is a rich source of fat?

(a) Almond (b) Cashew nut

(c) Walnut (d) Mango

Answers 46 (a) 47 (b) 48 (c) 49 (a) 50 (b)51 (a) 52 (a) 53 (c) 54 (c)

55. Which portion of the plant is considered free from viruses?

(a) Embryo (b) Xylum

(c) Cambium (d) Meristem

56. The crop richest in protein is

(a) Sunflower (b) Soyabean

(c) Peanut (d) Phaseolus

57. Optimum seed rate (g/ha) of Cauliflower is

(a) 300-400 (b) 500-700

(c) 700-800 (d) 800-900

58. Leaf curl virus of chilli is transmitted by

(a) White fly (b) Aphid

(c) Honey bees (d) Jassids

59. Kashmir beauty and Golden heart are the varieties of

(a) Radish (b) Carrot

(c) Beet root (d) Turnip

60. Garlic contains which organo sulphur compound?
(a) Alliin (b) Allicin
(c) Allinage (d) Diallyl disulphide

61. White grub beetles lay eggs
(a) On the underside of the leaf (b) On the plant stem at the level of ground
(c) Within the floral parts (d) Singly in sandy soil upto the depth of 10 cm

62. Yellow mosaic virus disease of moongbean is transmitted by
(a) *Bemisia tabaci* (b) *Aphis crassivora*
(c) N*ephotettix viruscens* (d) *Aphis gossypii*

63. Pink boll worm is a serious pest of
(a) Mustard (b) Cotton
(c) Gram (d) Pea

Answers 55 (d) 56 (b) 57 (a) 58 (b) 59 (b) 60 (b) 61 (d) 62 (b) 63 (b)

64. Pheromone trap attracts
(a) Female bugs (b) Catterpillars
(c) Female moths (d) Male moths

65. Which of the following is not a bio-pesticide?
(a) Bioneem (b) Biolep
(c) Carbaryl (d) Dipel

66. Which is a carbamate pesticide?
(a) Aldicarb (b) Heptachlor
(c) Malathion (d) Endosulphau

67. The worker honey bee is
(a) Drone (b) Sterile male
(c) Sterile female (d) None

68. Following is an example of Bt transgenic cotton
(a) Jayadhar (b) Varalaxmi
(c) NH-44 (d) Bollgaurd

69. Use of light trap for the management of pest is an example of
(a) Cultural control (b) Legal method of control
(c) Biological control (d) Mechanical method of control

70. The dwelling place of termite is also known as
(a) Canal (b) Tunnel
(c) Mound (d) Cave

71. The insecticide which is used in mosquito mat is
(a) Endosulphan (b) Diazinon
(c) Malathion (d) Allethrin

72. Munga silkworm belongs to the family
(a) Curculionidae (b) Formicidae
(c) Saturniidae (d) None

Answers 64(d) 65 (c) 66 (a) 67 (c) 68 (d) 69 (d)70 (c) 71 (d) 72 (c)

73. A disease not prevalent throughout the country, continent or world is known as
(a) Endemic (b) Epidemic
(c) Sporadic (d) Pandemic

74. Who is considered father of plant virology?
(a) Beijerinch (b) AE Mayer
(c) WM Stanley (d) Diener

75. Loose smut of wheat is
(a) Externally seed borne (b) Internally seed borne
(c) Both (a) and (b) (d) None of the above

76. Tea rust is caused by
(a) MLO (b) Virus
(c) Fungus (d) Algae

77. Panama wilt is a disease of
(a) Bamboo (b) Mango
(c) Pineapple (d) Banana

78. Which of the following is not a disease of apple?
(a) Bird eye (b) Powdery Mildew
(c) Downey mildew (d) Bunchy top

79. Most widely used fungicide for smut fungi is
(a) Vitavax (b) Plantvax
(c) Dithane M-45 (d) Sulfex

80. Race specific resistance is called
(a) Vertical Resistance (b) Horizontal resistance
(c) Adult plant resistance (d) Apparent resistance

81. Which fungicide is used against downy mildew?

(a) Karathane (b) Metalaxyl

(c) Oxathius (d) Bavistin

Answers 73 (c) 74 (c) 75 (b) 76 (d) 77 (d) 78 (d) 79 (a) 80 (a) 81 (b)

82. Rosette of apple is the deficiency symptom of

(a) Fe (b) Cl

(c) Mo (d) Zn

83. The end product of glycolysis is

(a) Glucose (b) Sucrose

(c) Pyruvic acid (d) None

84. World Standard Day is celebrated on

(a) 14th January (b) 14th October

(c) 14th November (d) 14th December

85. National income generated by agriculture is calculated by using

(a) Income method (b) Output method

(c) Expenditure method (d) Both (a) and (b)

86. 'Giffen' goods refer to

(a) Stock of goods (b) Inferior goods

(c) Lack of goods (d) Superior goods

87. Government of India signed WTO agreement

(a) 1981 (b) 1994

(c) 1995 (d) 1997

88. The first KVK was established at

(a) Nagpur (b) Pondichery

(c) Ludhiana (d) Jammu Tawi

89. The classical gene-for-gene hypothesis was proposed by

(a) Flor, 1956 (b) Painte, 1951

(c) Robinson, 1969 (d) Hayes, 1947

90. 'A' form of DNA has

(a) 10 base pairs/turn (b) 12 base pairs/turn

(c) 11 base pairs/turn (d) 9.33 base pairs/turn

Answers 82 (d) 83 (c) 84 (b) 85 (b) 86 (b) 87 (b) 88 (b) 89 (a) 90 (a)

91. 'Tetrazolin test' is used for
   (a) Testing seed viability
   (b) Membrane permeability test of seed
   (c) Estimation of amino acid in seed
   (d) Phospholipid determination of seed

92. Which one of the following crops do not belong to often allogamous species group?
   (a) Tomato
   (b) Sorghum
   (c) Cotton
   (d) Tobacco

93. The influence of more than one trait by a single gene in called
   (a) Polygene
   (b) Polytene
   (c) Pleiotropy
   (d) Phototroph

94. The pair of characters used in Pea by Mendel during his experiments were
   (a) Six
   (b) Eight
   (c) Nine
   (d) Seven

95. Which one of the following are nonsense codons?
   (a) UUA, AUG, UUU
   (b) UAC, UUG, UGC
   (c) UAA, UAG, UGA
   (d) UTA, UTG, UGT

96. The term gene was coined by
   (a) Mendel
   (b) Shull
   (c) Bateson
   (d) Johannsen

97. The chromosomes are most condensed at
   (a) Prophase
   (b) Anaphase
   (c) Metaphase
   (d) Telophase

98. Seed multiplication ratio in Paddy is
   (a) 1 : 100
   (b) 1 : 40
   (c) 1 : 80
   (d) 1 : 10

99. Land races are
   (a) Advanced Strains
   (b) Local varieties
   (c) Hybrid varieties
   (d) All of these

Answers 91 (a) 92 (a) 93 (c) 94 (d) 95 (c) 96 (d) 97 (c) 98 (c) 99 (b)

100. Inbred lines in maize are maintained by
   (a) Self pollination
   (b) Cross pollination
   (c) Open pollination
   (d) Sib pollination

101. The science that considers soil as a medium for plant growth is known as

(a) Pedology (b) Geology
(c) Edaphology (d) Soil Science

102. The nutrient that plant directly absorbs from air is

(a) C (b) N
(c) Cl (d) S

103. Most part of nitrogen is taken by plants in the following form

(a) NO_2 (b) NO_3
(c) NH_4+ (d) N

104. The elements which readily form metallic bonds are known as

(a) Chalcophile (b) Lithophile
(c) Atmosphile (d) Siderophile

105. Main constituent of sandstone is

(a) CaO (b) Al_2O_3
(c) SiO_2 (d) H_2O

106. Which one is the macronutrient?

(a) Fe (b) B
(c) S (d) Cu

107. Which one is the expanding type mineral?

(a) Pyrite (b) Dolomite
(c) Gypsum (d) Smectite

108. In general, in India Organic matter content in soil increases from

(a) East to West (b) West to East
(c) South to North (d) North to South

Answers 100 (a) 101 (c) 102 (b) 103 (b) 104 (d) 105 (c) 106 (c) 107 (d) 108 (c)

109. Which one of the following is most suitable for its use in agriculture?

(a) FYM (b) Straw
(c) Sawdust (d) Dead bodies of the microorganisms

110. In summer widest cracks are seen in

(a) Vertisol (b) Mollisol
(c) Alfisol (d) Ultisol

111. Correct sequence of the minerals in order to increase in resistance to weathering is
   (a) Dolomite, Gypsum, Gibsite, Calcite
   (b) Calcite, Dolomite, Gypsum, Gibsite
   (c) Gibsite, Dolomite, Calcite, Gypsum
   (d) Gypsum, Calcite, Dolomite, Gibsite

112. Rate of decomposition is fastest for
   (a) Cellulose (b) Sugar
   (c) Hemicellulose (d) Fats

113. Which is the most fertile soil?
   (a) Mollisol (b) Ultisol
   (c) Alfisol (d) Inceptisol

114. Potential evapotranspiration is measured by
   (a) Floating pan (b) Rain gauge
   (c) Stevenson's screen (d) Lysimeter

115. If the root/shoot ratio is greater, there will be more
   (a) Absorption (b) Transpiration
   (c) Reflection (d) Transmission

116. Headquarters of 'All India Soil and Land Use Survey' Organization is situated at
   (a) Mumbai (b) Delhi
   (c) Kolkata (d) Nagpur

117. Soil profile is defined as
   (a) Vertical section up to a depth of 30 cm
   (b) Vertical section up to a depth of 1 meter
   (c) Vertical section up to Regolith
   (d) Vertical section up to parent material

Answers 109 (a) 110 (a) 111 (b) 112 (b) 113 (a) 114 (d) 115 (b) 116 (b) 117 (d)

118. Group of soils developed from same parent material in similar climate and vegetation but that differ in relief are called
   (a) Toposequence (b) Catena
   (c) Climosequence (d) Podzols

119. Physical process of soil formation is
   (a) Oxidation (b) Nitrification
   (c) Hydrolysis (d) Transportation

120. 'E' horizon is characteristic of
   (a) Laterites (b) Podzols
   (c) Chernozems (d) Chestnuts

Answers 118 (b) 119 (d) 120 (b)

Combined Competitive (Preliminary) Examination, 2012

1. The contribution of agriculture towards the national income (recent) is about
   (a) 35—45% (b) < 27%
   (c) 45—70% (d) > 75%

2. The average rainfall of India is
   (a) 90 cm (b) 125 cm
   (c) 750 cm (d) 112 cm

3. Which monsoon of India contributes maximum rainfall in the country?
   (a) Post monsoon (b) Winter monsoon
   (c) South-west monsoon (d) North-east monsoon

4. The State of India having highest area under rice crop is
   (a) Bihar (b) Punjab
   (c) Kerala (d) West Bengal

5. The State of India having highest productivity of groundnut is
   (a) Gujarat (b) M.P.
   (c) Maharashtra (d) Andhra Pradesh

6. Total pulse production in India is maximum in
   (a) U.P. (b) M.P.
   (c) Punjab (d) Tamil Nadu

7. The maximum production of wheat is in
   (a) Maharashtra (b) Punjab
   (c) M.P. (d) U.P.

8. The sowing time of the Boro rice grown in West Bengal is
   (a) May-June (b) June-July
   (c) January-February (d) September-October

9. Recommended depth of sowing for dwarf wheat varieties is

(a) 5 cm (b) 9 cm

(c) 3 cm (d) 7.5 cm

Answers 1 (b) 2 (b) 3 (c) 4 (d) 5 (a) 6 (b) 7 (d) 8 (c) 9 (a)

10. The conversion factor to convert % P to % P_2O_5 is

(a) 1.29 (b) 2.90

(c) 2.29 (d) 0.43

11. The seed rate of desi gram (chick-pea) crop should be

(a) 50 to 60 kg per ha (b) 60 to 90 kg per ha

(c) 90 to 120 kg per ha (d) 100 to 110 kg per ha

12. The row to row distance of long duration arhar (pigeon-pea) varieties is 75 cm and plant to plant distance is

(a) 25 to 30 cm (b) 40 to 45 cm

(c) 10 to 12 cm (d) 15 to 18 cm

13. For weed control of Urad (Black gram) hand weeding should be given at .... days after sowing.

(a) 25—30 (b) 40—50

(c) 50—55 (d) 15—20

14. The best time of sowing for field pea crop in north India is

(a) 15 to 25 October (b) 10 to 25 November

(c) 5 to 10 October (d) 25 to 30 November

15. The optimum seed rate of small seeded varieties of lentil crop is

(a) 15 to 20 kg per ha (b) 35 to 40 kg per ha

(c) 40 to 50 kg per ha (d) None of these

16. Soybean is a

(a) Short day plant (b) Long day plant

(c) Day-neutral plant (d) All of these

17. The row to row distance of spreading type groundnut crop should be

(a) 30 cm (b) 45 cm

(c) 55 cm (d) 20 cm

18. The most essential stages for irrigation in Sarson (mustard) is/are

(a) Flowering stage (b) Fruiting stage

(c) Early growth stage (d) All of above

Answers 10 (c) 11 (b) 12 (a) 13 (d) 14 (b) 15 (b) 16 (a) 17 (b) 18 (a)

19. Seed rate of sesame is

(a) 3 to 5 kg per ha (b) 2 to 3 kg per ha

(c) 8 to 10 kg per ha (d) 10 to 15 kg per ha

20. The nitrogen requirement for one hectare of linseed under irrigated conditions will be about

(a) 50 to 60 kg (b) 60 to 90 kg

(c) 40 to 45 kg (d) None of these

21. Which crop(s) is/are sown as intercrop in October sown sugarcane?

(a) Wheat (b) Brassica

(c) Radish (d) All of above

22. The most suitable soil for cotton cultivation in India is

(a) Red soil (b) Laterite soil

(c) Hill soil (d) Black soil

23. The most critical stage/s for irrigation in potato is/are

(a) Stolon formation stage (b) Tuberization stage

(c) 25% tuber formation stage (d) All of these

24. As per principles of crop rotation, legume should be included in rotation because

(a) it increases the total pulse production

(b) emphasis has been given on pulses production

(c) it helps in maintenance of soil fertility

(d) it increases cropping intensity

25. Which one of the following is a variety of wheat crop?

(a) PR-116 (b) PBW550

(c) PMH-1 (d) SML668

26. Growing of a crop in between two rows of another crop is known as

(a) Inter cropping (b) Mixed cropping

(c) Multiple cropping (d) Intensive cropping

27. Growing of more than two crops in a year in the same field is known as

(a) Mixed cropping (b) Multiple cropping

(c) Relay cropping (d) Inter cropping

Answers 19 (a) 20 (b) 21 (d) 22 (d) 23 (d) 24 (c) 25 (b) 26 (a) 27 (b)

28. Growing of two or more than two crops in a field in the same season is called as
    (a) Mixed farming (b) Multiple cropping
    (c) Mixed cropping (d) Relay cropping

29. A well developed soil has
    (a) A horizon (b) B horizon
    (c) C horizon (d) All of these

30. What fraction of soil nitrogen is present in inorganic form ?
    (a) 1 to 5% (b) < 1%
    (c) 7% (d) 10%

31. A soil is said to be medium in organic matter if organic matter content is
    (a) 0.86 to 1.29% (b) 1.29 to 2%
    (c) 0.86 to 1% (d) 0.5 to 0.9%

32. Mineralization of nitrogen refers to the conversion of
    (a) Organic form into inorganic form
    (b) Inorganic form into organic form
    (c) Organic form to nitrogenous compound
    (d) All of these

33. The carbon content of organic matter is
    (a) 40% (b) 32%
    (c) 58% (d) 68%

34. Which nutrient is applied in large quantity for raising the cereal field crops?
    (a) Nitrogen (b) Potash
    (c) Phosphorus (d) Sulphur

35. Bulk density of normal soil is
    (a) 1.33 g/cc (b) 1.8 g/cc
    (c) 2.66 g/cc (d) < 1.0 g/cc

36. The quantity of urea required to supply 120 kg N/ha is
    (a) 120 kg (b) 240 kg
    (c) 260 kg (d) 60 kg

Answers 28 (c) 29 (d) 30 (b) 31 (a) 32 (a) 33 (c) 34 (a) 35 (b) 36 (c)

37. The pH range of sodic soil is
    (a) 6.6 to 7.3 (b) 6.0 to 8.0
    (c) 7.0 to 8.0 (d) 8.5 to 10.5

38. Generally C.N. ratio of normal soil is

(a) 10 : 1 (b) 15 : 1
(c) 16 : 1 (d) 5 : 1

39. Bacteria present in the root nodules of legumes plants is

(a) Clostridium (b) Azospirillum
(c) Rhizobium (d) Azotobacter

40. Rhizosphere refers to the small area

(a) Around the root (b) On the root
(c) Near the primary root (d) All of these

41. The enzyme responsible for the conversion of molecular nitrogen into NH3 is

(a) Nitrogenase (b) Urease
(c) Aminase (d) Nuclease

42. When organic matter with C : P ratio greater than 300 : 1 is added in soil then net .... will take place.

(a) Mineralization (b) Immobilization
(c) Both of these (d) None of these

43. Muriate of potash is more effective in .... soils.

(a) Saline (b) Neutral
(c) Alkaline (d) Acidic

44. If the soil contains 110 to 280 kg K2O per ha, then soil will be .... in this regard.

(a) High (b) Low
(c) Very high (d) Medium

45. The conversion of ammonia into nitrate by micro-organisms is known as.........

(a) Nitrogen fixation (b) Nitrification
(c) Denitrification (d) Loss of nitrogen

Answers 37 (d) 38 (a) 39 (c) 40 (a) 41 (a) 42 (b) 43 (d) 44 (d) 45 (b)

46. Which micronutrient is maximum available in the soil?

(a) Fe (b) Bo
(c) Zn (d) Cu

47. Which of the following fertilizer has maximum number of primary plant nutrients?

(a) DAP (b) TSP
(c) Murate of Potash (d) Ammonium nitrate

48. The fertilizers which have two or more than two major plant nutrients in their chemical compound form are called.........

(a) Double fertilizer (b) Complex fertilizer
(c) Mixed fertilizer (d) Organic fertilizer

49. The ratio between CO2 produced and O2 consumed indicates ....

(a) Respiration ratio (b) Energy ratio
(c) Respiration quotient (d) None of these

50. C6H12O6 → 2C2H5OH + 2CO2—17 K Cal energy. The reaction indicates ....

(a) Anaerobic respiration (b) Aerobic respiration
(c) Photosynthesis (d) None of these

51. Ascorbic acid is.........

(a) Enzyme (b) Vitamin
(c) Hormone (d) Mineral

52. Which of the following restricts coverage of wheat in India?

(a) Photoperiod (b) Temperature
(c) Light intensity (d) Irrigation

53. Transportation of water to different plant parts is done by.........

(a) Xylem cells (b) Phloem cells
(c) Both of these (d) None of these

54. One atmosphere pressure can pull the water in plant cells up to....... (approximately).

(a) 100 feet (b) 200 feet
(c) 30 feet (d) 5 feet

Answers 46 (a) 47 (a) 48 (b) 49 (c) 50 (a) 51 (b) 52 (d) 53 (a) 54 (c)

55. When plant cells are fully turgid, then.........

(a) OP = TP (b) OP = DPD
(c) Both of these (d) None of these

56. Under the plasmolysis condition,.........

(a) OP = TP (b) DPD = OP
(c) DPD = TP (d) DPD = Zero

57. The water loss through transpiration during the whole life of maize plant is about....

(a) 100 litres (b) 200 litres
(c) 400 litres (d) 500 litres

58. How much percent of total area of leaf in field crops is covered by stomata?

(a) 5 to 10% (b) 10 to 15%

(c) 1 to 2% (d) None of these

59. During the photosynthesis, the light .... colour(s) which is/are absorbed to the maximum.

(a) Yellow (b) Green

(c) Blue and red (d) All of these

60. If relative humidity of atmosphere is low, then transpiration rate will be.........

(a) More (b) Less

(c) Remains same (d) None of these

61. In active uptake of nutrients by plant,.........

(a) Energy will be required (b) No energy will be required

(c) Both of these (d) Cannot be said

62. Downward translocation of nutrients occurs by.........

(a) Xylem cells (b) Phloem cells

(c) Both of these (d) None of these

63. Which of the following controls the cell elongation, apical dominance, root initiation

(a) Gibberellins (b) Abscisic acid

(c) Auxins (d) Ethylene

Answers 55 (a) 56 (b) 57 (b) 58 (c) 59 (c) 60 (a) 61 (a) 62 (b) 63 (c)

64. Under the deficiency of ...., the new leaves turn yellow, roots and stems become abnormally long and develop woodiness.

(a) Fe (b) P

(c) K (d) S

65. In the deficiency of……, the older leaves of the plants become yellowish or pale green.

(a) N (b) P

(c) K (d) Mg

66. The term genetics was coined by.........

(a) Charles Darwin (b) Lamarck

(c) Mendel (d) Bateson

67. Segregation occurs during.........
    (a) Mitosis (b) Endomitosis
    (c) Meiosis (d) All of these

68. In a genome, each type of chromosome is represented.........
    (a) Only once (b) Twice
    (c) Thrice (d) Many times

69. The term heterosis was coined by.........
    (a) East (1908) (b) Davenport (1908)
    (c) Shull (1914) (d) Jones (1917)

70. The science which is used for genetic improvement of crop plants is referred to as....
    (a) Plant breeding (b) Science of crop improvement
    (c) Crop improvement technology (d) All of these

71. Self pollination is a form of.........
    (a) Inbreeding (b) Outbreeding
    (c) Random mating (d) None of these

72. Homozygous population includes.........
    (a) Pure lines (b) Inbred lines
    (c) Multi lines (d) All of these

Answers 64 (d) 65 (a) 66 (d) 67 (d) 68 (a) 69 (c) 70 (a) 71 (a) 72 (d)

73. Hybrid progeny from a cross between two inbreds is known as.........
    (a) Single cross hybrid (b) Double cross hybrid
    (c) Three way cross hybrid (d) Multiple cross hybrid

74. Synthetic variety is constituted/synthesized by mixing.........
    (a) All possible crosses among inbreds with good gca
    (b) Several pure lines
    (c) Several open pollinated genotypes
    (d) Several inbred lines

75. Indian Institute of Sugarcane Research is located at.........
    (a) Coimbatore (b) Kanpur
    (c) Lucknow (d) Sholapur

76. Directorate of Rapeseed and Mustard Research is located at.........
    (a) Kanpur (b) Bharatpur
    (c) Hissar (d) Varanasi

77. Single seed descent method was first proposed by.........

(a) Goulden (1939) (b) Grafius (1965)

(c) Thoday (1960) (d) Mather (1953)

78. Sum total of genes in a species is called.........

(a) Genetic diversity (b) Genetic variability

(c) Gene pool (d) Gene bank

79. Which of the following is cool season crop?

(a) Potato (b) Cucumber

(c) Bean (d) Pumpkin

80. Which of the following is warm season crop?

(a) Cabbage (b) Potato

(c) Tomato (d) Pea

81. Alternate bearing is most common in.........

(a) Citrus (b) Mango

(c) Papaya (d) Guava

Answers 73 (a) 74 (a) 75 (c) 76 (b) 77 (a) 78 (c) 79 (a) 80 (c) 81 (b)

82. The depth of pits for orchard plantation should generally be.........

(a) 1 meter (b) ½ meter

(c) 5 meters (d) 2 meters

83. The filler tree in mango orchard is.........

(a) Ber (b) Papaya

(c) Apple (d) Litchi

84. The seed rate for onion should be.........

(a) 5 kg/ha (b) 18 kg/ha

(c) 10 to 12 kg/ha (d) 1 to 2 kg/ha

85. The yield of tomato (tonnes/ha) is.........

(a) 40 to 45 (b) 20 to 25

(c) 10 to 15 (d) 50 to 55

86. Snow ball-16 is a variety of.........

(a) Cauliflower (b) Cabbage

(c) Potato (d) Tomato

87. In fruits and vegetables, waxing is done to reduce.........

(a) Transpiration (b) Respiration

(c) Both (a) and (b) (d) None of these

88. Pectin is the most important ingredient in the preparation of.........

(a) Jam (b) Jelly

(c) Murabba (d) Candy

89. Fruit ripening hormone is.........

(a) Ethrel (b) Auxin

(c) GA3 (d) None of these

90. By which of the following treatment, the wilt disease of gram crop can be controlled?

(a) Deep ploughing and late sowing (b) Treating seeds with fungicides

(c) BHC (d) All of these

Answers 82 (a) 83(b) 84(c) 85 (b) 86 (a) 87 (c) 88 (b) 89 (a) 90 (d)

91. Which of the following is an example of biological pest control?

(a) Use of pesticides (b) Parasitic insects

(c) Environmental effect (d) None of these

92. High volume spraying is that in which we can give complete coverage to one hectare crop with more than .... litre of liquid.

(a) 1000 (b) 1500

(c) 100 (d) 250

93. Late blight of potato can be controlled by.........

(a) BHC dust 5% (b) Bordeux mixture 4 : 4 : 50

(c) DDT (d) All of these

94. Which of the following is/are systemic fungicide(s)?

(a) Vitavax (b) Benlate

(c) Bristol (d) All of these

95. Which of the following types of insecticides are used against food grain pests in storage?

(a) Organic insecticides (b) Fumigants

(c) Inorganic insecticides (d) All of these

96. Host resistance and insect-disease belong to which one of the following pest control measures?

(a) Natural control (b) Physical control

(c) Chemical control (d) Biological control

97. Flooding and drying for pest control is.........

(a) Natural control (b) Physical control

(c) Cultural control (d) None of these

98. Seed born and soil born diseases can be controlled by.........

(a) Organo-mercurials (b) Copper fungicides

(c) Copper sulphates (d) Zinc sulphates

99. The cost which do vary with the output is called.........

(a) Average variable cost (b) Average fixed cost

(c) Variable cost (d) None of these

Answers 91(b) 92 (a) 93 (b) 94 (b) 95 (d) 96 (a) 97 (c) 98 (b) 99 (c)

100. Which of the following is not considered as component of farm business?

(a) Capital (b) Land

(c) Environment (d) Management

101. In India first State Agricultural University was established at.........

(a) Ludhiana (b) Banglore

(c) Pantnagar (d) Anand

102. Short term loans are mainly given for the purchase of.........

(a) Seeds (b) Bullocks

(c) Pumpset (d) Heavy machinery

103. A small garden or keeping few birds with the main enterprise is known as.........

(a) Supplementary enterprise (b) complementary enterprise

(c) Major enterprise (d) competitive enterprise

104. Which of the following is an economic factor affecting the type or system of farming?

(a) Availability of capital (b) Water

(c) Land (d) All of these

105. The owner of land in state farming is.........

(a) Farmer (b) Government

(c) Capitalist (d) None of these

106. The basic objective of extension education is.........

(a) Development of the people of BDO

(b) Development of the people in general

(c) Development of the relatives of Pradhan

(d) none of these

107. Effective extension service is a process of.........

(a) Helping the people to help themselves
(b) Profiting the local leaders
(c) Helping the BDO
(d) All of these

108. After a suitable extension teaching, the villagers attain desirable changes in their.........

(a) Behaviour (b) Habits
(c) Health (d) All of these

Answers 100 (c) 101(c) 102 (a) 103(a) 104 (d) 105 (b) 106 (b) 107 (a) 108 (d)

109. Which of the following body(ies) is/are responsible for development at base level?

(a) Block (b) Panchayat
(c) District (d) All of these

110. A farmer, which has land holding between 1 to 2 hectare, is known as.........

(a) Marginal farmer (b) Optimal farmer
(c) Small farmer (d) Big farmer

111. Diversified farming is a kind of ....

(a) System of farming (b) Type of farming
(c) Both of these (d) None of these

112. Which of the following is not a method of group communication?

(a) Conferences (b) Field trips
(c) National demonstrations (d) Farm and home visits

113. The pilot project in rural development was started in 1948 at.........

(a) Etawah (b) Patna
(c) Gurgaon (d) Ludhiana

114. Panchayat Raj System was established in India in the year.........

(a) 1958 (b) 1959
(c) 1947 (d) 1950

115. Maximum variability is found in.........

(a) F1 generation (b) F2 generation
(c) F3 generation (d) F4 generation

116. Which of the following is used to control soil pests?

(a) Endrin (b) Aldrin

(c) Malathion (d) Parathion

117. Which of the following variety of rice is a cross between IR262 and TKM6 evolved at IRRI, Philippines?

(a) IR 8 (b) Pusa 2-21

(c) IR 20 (d) Ratna

Answers 109 (b) 110 (c) 111(c) 112 (d) 113 (a) 114 (a) 115 (b) 116 (b) 117 (c)

118. Which of the following is a growth retardant ?

(a) Alar (b) GA 4

(c) IBA (d) Kinetin

119. Which of the following selections is used in potato improvement?

(a) Hybridization (b) Clonal selection

(c) Pure line selection (d) Mass selection

120. PBW 343 is a popular variety of.........

(a) Rice (b) Maize

(c) Barley (d) Wheat

Answers 118 (a) 119 (b) 120 (d)

Combined Competitive (Preliminary) Examination, 2011

1. Substitution haploids are referred to as:
   (a) n+1 (b) n-1
   (c) n-1+1 (d) n+2
2. A cross of F_1 with its homozygous recessive parent is known as:
   (a) Back cross (b) Reciprocal cross
   (c) Test cross (d) Top cross
3. When value is expressed in terms of money, it is called:
   (a) Price (b) Cost
   (c) Service (d) Goods
4. The difference between the price paid by the consumer and the price received by the producer is known as:
   (a) Marketing efficiency (b) Price-spread
   (c) Marketing cost (d) Marketing integration
5. A bale of cotton weights:
   (a) 70 Kg (b) 100 Kg
   (c) 170 Kg (d) 190 Kg
6. The chromosome theory of inheritance was first postulated by:
   (a) Avery, McCarty and Mcleod (b) Morgan and Sturtevant
   (c) Sutton and Boveri (d) Frederick Griffth
7. Treatment of fruits and vegetables with hot water for a short period of time prior to canning is known as:
   (a) Breathing (b) Hot pealing
   (c) Bleaching (d) Blanching

8. Which one of the phytohormones control the apical dominance in plants?
   (a) Auxin (b) Cytokinin
   (c) Ethylene (d) Giberellin

9. Kharif, Rabi and Zaid words belong to:
   (a) Urdu (b) Persian
   (c) Arabic (d) French

Answers 1 (c) 2 (c) 3 (a) 4 (b) 5 (c) 6 (c) 7 (d) 8 (a) 9 (c)

10. Bee keeping and rearing for honey production is known as:
   (a) Sericulture (b) Apiculture
   (c) Silviculture (d) Olericulture

11. Which is the growth regulator which promotes fruit ripening?
   (a) GA_3 (b) Ethylene
   (c) Auxin (d) Cytokinin

12. Fruit drop is controlled by:
   (a) IBA (b) NAA
   (c) IAA (d) GA_3

13. It is an important variety of cluster bean:
   (a) Pusa Falguni (b) Pusa Basmati
   (c) Pusa Nasdar (d) Pusa Navbahar

14. Synthetic variety is developed by:
   (a) Crossing inbred lines tested for GCA
   (b) Mixing seed of inbred lines
   (c) Crossing inbreed lines tested for SCA
   (d) Mixing seeds of open pollinated cultivars

15. Which one of the following process is most adversely affected by the deficiency of magnesium?
   (a) Defoliation (b) Upward translocation of nutrients
   (c) Downward movement of nutrients (d) Photosynthesis and carbohydrate metabolism

16. Development of fruit without fertilization is known as:
   (a) Polyembryony (b) Parthenocarpy
   (c) Apomixis (d) Sporogenesis

17. The Mexican wheat varieties introduced in India in 1963 were:
    (a) Kayan Sona and Sonalika (b) S 308 and K 68
    (c) Lerma Rojo and Sonera 64 (d) HD 1982 and HD 2122

18. Initial seed of an improved variety is called
    (a) Nuclear seed (b) Foundation seed
    (c) Breeder seed (d) Certified seed

Answers 10 (b) 11 (b) 12 (b) 13 (a) 14 (a) 15 (d) 16 (b) 17 (a) 18 (a)

19. Who developed world's first cotton hybrid?
    (a) NGP Rao (b) B.P. Paul
    (c) C.T. Patel (d) D.S. Athwal

20. The molecular model of DNA was proposed by:
    (a) Miescher (b) Punnet and square
    (c) Chargaff (d) Watson and Crick

21. Powdery mildew disease is caused by:
    (a) Bacteria (b) Virus
    (c) Fungus (d) Nematode

22. Solar energy treatment of wheat seed is recommended for the control of:
    (a) Loose smut (b) Hill bunt
    (c) Black rust (d) Karnal bunt

23. Lime is used for reclamation of:
    (a) Acidic soil (b) Alkaline soil
    (c) Calcareous soil (d) None of these

24. Tomato and cotton plants are:
    (a) Short day plants (b) Day neutral plants
    (c) Long day plants (d) None of these

25. Transpiration will be maximum when soil is:
    (a) Wet and atmosphere is dry (b) Dry and atmosphere is humid
    (c) Wet and atmosphere is humid (d) Dry and atmosphere is dry

26. Which of the following is a unit less measure of dispersion?
    (a) Standard deviation (b) Coefficient of variation
    (c) Mean deviation (d) Range

27. Which of the following is not related to extension education?

(a) Heterogeneous learners (b) Vertical teaching

(c) Horizontal teaching (d) Voluntary participation

Answers 19 (c) 20 (d) 21 (c) 22 (a) 23 (a) 24 (b) 25 (a) 26 (b) 27 (b)

28. For commercial cultivation of Banana which type of sucker is used?

(a) Sward sucker (b) Slips

(c) Water sucker (d) Crown

29. Replication of DNA occurs during:

(a) Metaphase (b) Telophase

(c) Interphase (d) Anaphase

30. PCR refers to

(a) Polymearse chain reaction (b) Poly clonal response

(c) Poly coloured raddish (d) Partially controlled reaction

31. GMO means:

(a) Genetically mutated oats (b) Genetically modified organism

(c) General Micro organism (d) Genetics of micro organisms

32. Centres of origin for different crops were given by:

(a) Aristotle (b) Darwin

(c) N.I. Vavilov (d) G.H. Shull

33. Alternative form of a gene is known as:

(a) Allele (b) Genome

(c) Pseudo-allele (d) Iso-allele

34. Which blood group is considered as universal recipient?

(a) B (b) A

(c) AB (d) O

35. Who gave the term heterosis?

(a) Johnson (b) Mendel

(c) Davenport (d) Shull

36. Which estimates of heterosis is of commercial or practical value?

(a) Average heterosis (b) Heterobeltiosis

(c) Economic heterosis (d) Luxuriance

Answers 28 (a) 29 (c) 30 (a) 31 (b) 32 (c) 33 (a) 34 (c) 35 (d) 36 (c)

37. Jaya and Ratna rice varieties contain the dwarfing genes from

(a) Dee-geo-woo-gen (b) Norin 8

(c) Spontaneous mutation (d) Induced mutation

38. IR 8 varieties of Rice was developed at

(a) CRRI Cuttack (b) IRRI, Philippines

(c) Taiwan (d) Japan

39. The term nobilization is related to

(a) Wheat (b) Rice

(c) Sugarcane (d) Soyabean

40. *Helminthosporium maydis* causes southern leaf blight in

(a) Wheat (b) Maize

(c) Barley (d) Rice

41. Hybrid seed production in Jowar and Bajra is based on:

(a) A, B and R lines (b) A and B lines

(c) A and R lines (d) B and R lines

42. General combining ability (GCA) can be estimated from the performance of:

(a) Parents (b) Back cross

(c) F_1s (d) F_2s

43. The term yellow revolution is related to:

(a) Maize (b) Fruits

(c) Oil seeds (d) Vegetables

44. Tag of which colour is used for breeder seed?

(a) Yellow/golden (b) White

(c) Blue (d) Green

45. The maximum heterosis is likely to be manifested in

(a) Double cross (b) Single cross

(c) Three way cross (d) Double top cross

Answers 37 (a) 38 (b) 39 (c) 40 (b) 41 (c) 42 (c) 43 (c) 44 (a) 45 (a)

46. Potato, coffee and alfaalfa are:

(a) Diploids (b) Allopolyploids

(c) Segmental allopolyploids (d) Auto polyploids

47. Botanical name of apple is:

(a) *Prunus amygelalus* (b) *Prunus persica*

(c) *Malus pumila* (d) *Malus persica*

48. The quickest method for developing an improved variety is:
(a) Primary introduction (b) Mass selection
(c) Secondary introduction (d) Domestication

49. Rice flower has how many stamens?
(a) 6 (b) 4
(c) 3 (d) 8

50. Cleistogamy promotes:
(a) Cross-pollination (b) Self pollination
(c) Geitonogamy (d) All of the above

51. Johannsen developed pureline theory using the seeds of beans variety:
(a) Price (b) Princeton
(c) Century (d) Princess

52. Pusa Baisakhi is a variety of:
(a) Mung bean (b) Urd bean
(c) Rice bean (d) Cow pea

53. Isogenic lines are easily produced by which breeding method?
(a) Bulk (b) SSD
(c) Back cross (d) Pedigree

54. Leaf rust resistance in wheat (T-aestivum) has been transferred from:
(a) *Triticum monococcum* (b) *Triticum speltoides*
(c) *Triticum timopheevii* (d) All of the above

Answers 46 (d) 47 (c) 48 (b) 49 (a) 50 (b) 51 (d) 52 (a) 53 (c) 54 (d)

55. The chief weakness of single seed descent scheme is:
(a) Plant loss (b) Lack of opportunity for selection
(c) High demand on resources (d) Loss of high yielding segregants

56. Which of the following is a pest of apple?
(a) *Sylepta lunalis* (b) *Eriosoma lanigerum*
(c) *Cydia hemidoxa* (d) *Nodostoma subscotatum*

57. Simple recurrent selection is the most suited for character with:
(a) Low heritability (b) Moderate heritability
(c) High heritability (d) All of the above

58. Reciprocal recurrent selection allows selection for:
(a) GCA (b) SCA
(c) Improved population performance (d) All of the above

59. Knight used hybridization to develop popular varieties of:

(a) Apple (b) Apple, peach and grape

(c) Apple, peach and strawberry (d) All of the above

60. Selection for simply inherited trait is started from:

(a) F_2 (b) F_3

(c) F_4 (d) F_5

61. Who was awarded the Noble Peace prize in Agriculture?

(a) Dr. M.S. Swaminathan (b) Dr. Norman E. Borlaug

(c) Dr. V. Kurien (d) None of the above

62. The Union Minister of Agriculture in India is:

(a) Balram Jakhar (b) R.S. Paroda

(c) Sharad Pawar (d) None of the above

63. Lab to land programme has been launched in India to transfer:

(a) Ag. Technology to farmer's fields

(b) Ag. Methodology to farmer's fields

(c) Ag. Philosophy to farmer's fields

(d) Ag. Policy to farmer's fields

Answers 55 (a) 56 (b) 57 (c) 58 (d) 59 (d) 60 (a) 61 (b) 62 (c) 63 (a)

64. Opaque-2 gene increases lysine and tryptophan content and the protein quality in:

(a) Rice (b) Maize

(c) Wheat (d) Pearl millet

65. K.V.K. means:

(a) Kisan Vigyan Kendra (b) Krishi Vikas Kendra

(c) Krishi Vigyan Kendra (d) Kisan Vikas Kendra

66. Who is the Chairman of the Planning Commission?

(a) President (b) Vice-President

(c) Prime Minister (d) Home Minister

67. The highest share of agricultural commodity in export of India is that of:

(a) Rice (b) Cashew

(c) Sugarcane (d) Fruits

68. Practising agriculture without the use of Chemicals and Fertilizers is known as:

(a) Extensive farming (b) Intensive farming

(c) Inorganic farming (d) Organic farming

69. NABARD was established in the year:

(a) 1980 (b) 1981

(c) 1982 (d) 1983

70. A short duration crop in between two main crops is termed as:

(a) Catch crop (b) Cash crop

(c) Commercial crop (d) Companion crop

71. Maize surpasses all cereal crops in terms of:

(a) Area (b) Production

(c) Yield (d) Consumption

72. In India, share of agriculture in National Income is approximately:

(a) 45% (b) 25%

(c) 35% (d) 42%

Answers 64 (b) 65 (c) 66 (c) 67 (a) 68 (d) 69 (c) 70 (a) 71 (b) 72 (b)

73. The arrangement of soil particles in certain definite pattern is known as:

(a) Soil texture (b) Soil structure

(c) Soil aggregates (d) Soil parameter

74. Which of the fly is pest of cotton?

(a) Fruit fly (b) Stem fly

(c) Saw fly (d) White fly

75. Directorate of Plant protection, quarantine and storage is located at:

(a) Moradabad (b) Ahmedabad

(c) Faridabad (d) Allahabad

76. A pH value of 6.0 indicates that soil reaction is:

(a) Acidic (b) Alkaline

(c) Neutral (d) Highly alkaline

77. Oxygen is required by the plants for:

(a) Respiration (b) Transpiration

(c) Photosynthesis (d) Gutation

78. Which of the following is considered as bio-fertilizer?

(a) Farm yard manure (FYM) (b) Compost

(c) Green manure (d) Blue green algae

79. Apple belongs to family:

(a) Legminosae (b) Rosaceae

(c) Cruciferae (d) Liliaceae

80. The building block of cellulose is:

(a) Maltose (b) Glucose

(c) Fructose (d) Glucose + Fructose

81. The best soil amendment under alkaline condition is application of:

(a) Calcium (b) Phosphorus

(c) Gypsum (d) None

Answers 73 (b) 74 (d) 75 (c) 76 (a) 77 (a) 78 (d) 79 (b) 80 (b) 81 (c)

82. Which is the most appropriate cause of seedlessness in Banana?

(a) Triploidy (b) Parthenocarpy

(c) Monoecious condition (d) Lack of pollination

83. The theory of acquired characters was proposed by:

(a) Darwin (b) Lamarck

(c) Weismann (d) Mendel

84. The normal seed rate of wheat is

(a) 50 kg/ha (b) 75 kg/ha

(c) 100 kg/ha (d) 125 kg/ha

85. Which part of the walnut fruit is stony and woody?

(a) Epicarp (b) Endocarp

(c) Mesocarp (d) None of the above

86. Soil erosion increase with:

(a) No tillage (b) Ideal tillage

(c) Mulching (d) Excessive tillage

87. Pomegranate has been placed in which of the salt tolerant fruit trees?

(a) High (b) Medium

(c) Low (d) Very high

88. The science which deals with rearing of silkworm is known as:

(a) Apiculture (b) Vermiculture

(c) Sericulture (d) Agriculture

89. Principles of experimental design were given by:

(a) Wilcox (b) R.A. Fisher

(c) W.C. Cocharan (d) Cox and Cocharan

90. The bulk density of soil is always _____ than particle density.

(a) Higher (b) Lower

(c) Equal (d) Vey high

Answers 82 (a) 83 (b) 84 (c) 85 (b) 86 (d) 87 (b) 88 (c) 89 (b) 90 (b)

91. Which one of the following is not an aldose?

(a) Glucose (b) Galactose
(c) Mannoase (d) Fructose

92. Little leaf disease of Brinjal is caused by:

(a) Viroid (b) Virus
(c) Phytoplasma (d) Spiroplasma

93. A chromosome with median position of centromere is known as:

(a) Telocentric (b) Acentric
(c) Metacentric (d) Paracentric

94. The value of coefficient of correlation varies from:

(a) 0.0 to 1.0 (b) -- -1.0 to 1.0
(c) 1.0 to 10.0 (d) 10.0 to 100

95. The negative logrithum of H^+ ion is known as:

(a) pH (b) Salinity
(c) Solocity (d) Acidity

96. Technical name of Furadan 3 G is:

(a) Carbosulfan (b) Carbofuran
(c) Phorate (d) Sebufos

97. Sugarcane is________plant.

(a) C_3 (b) C_4
(c) CAM (d) None of above

98. Nitrogen is taken by the plants in form of:

(a) Nitrate (b) Element nitrogen
(c) Nitrite (d) Nitric acid

99. Allahabad Safeda is a variety of:

(a) Mango (b) Guava
(c) Fig (d) Orange

Answers 91 (d) 92 (c) 93 (c) 94 (b) 95 (a) 96 (b) 97 (b) 98 (a) 99 (b)

100. Which chemical is used in preparation of Insect Killing jar?

(a) NaCl (b) H_2SO_4
(c) CO_2 (d) KCN

101. Tetrasomic is represented as:

(a) 2n (b) 4n
(c) 2n+1 (d) 2n+2

102. Splitting of H_2O in the presence of light is termed as

(a) Photosynthesis (b) Photophasis
(c) Phototlysis (d) Photoperiodism

103. Mite possesses how many pair(s) of legs?

(a) One (b) Two
(c) Six (d) Four

104. The fertility restorer parent is represented as:

(a) R line (b) A line
(c) B line (d) Pure line

105. Thompson Seedless is a popular variety of:

(a) Water melon (b) Grape
(c) Guava (d) Banana

106. The plants which respond least to changed day length are known as:

(a) Day Neutral (b) Long Day
(c) Short day (d) None of these

107. The accumulation of soluble salts in the soil is known as:

(a) Alkalinization (b) Salinization
(c) Calcification (d) Acidifiation

108. Haploids plants can be obtained through:

(a) Shoot tip culture (b) Protoplast culture
(c) Somatic hybridization (d) Anther culture

Answers 100 (d) 101(d) 102 (c) 103 (d) 104 (a) 105(b) 106 (a) 107(b) 108 (d)

109. Genetic purity of seeds can be treated by:

(a) Germination test (b) Tetrazolium test
(c) Acetocarmine test (d) Grow out test

110. Which of the following pulses has the highest protein content?

(a) Pigeon pea (b) Green gram
(c) Soyabean (d) Black gram

111. Edible part of banana fruit is:

(a) Endosperm (b) Meso and Endocarp
(c) Endocarp only (d) Mesocarp only

112. The basic chromosome number of apple is:
(a) 34 (b) 68
(c) 17 (d) 51

113. The Science dealing with genesis, survey and classification of soils is known as:
(a) Taxonomy (b) Soil science
(c) Phenology (d) Pedology

114. Which of the following crops require water logging condition?
(a) Sugarcane (b) Cotton
(c) Paddy (d) Maize

115. At what stem length the rose flowers must be cut at tight bud stage for export?
(a) 60 (b) 20
(c) 80 (d) 40

116. Which type of herbicide 2,4 –D is?
(a) Non-selective (b) Selective
(c) Toxic (d) Non-toxic

117. The main site of respiration in plants cells is:
(a) Chloroplasts (b) Mitochondria
(c) Lysosomes (d) Ribosomes

Answers 109 (d) 110 (c) 111(d) 112(c) 113(d) 114 (c) 115 (a) 116 (b) 117 (b)

118. Meiosis is also referred to as:
(a) Equational division (b) Reduction division
(c) Homotypic division (d) Assymertic division

119. B-Chromosomes are also known as:
(a) Accessory chromosomes (b) Extra Chromosomes
(c) Supernumerary chromosomes (d) All of the above

120. Brassica juncea is an amphidiploid between:
(a) *B. campestris* × *B. nigra* (b) *B. campestris* × *B. oleracea*
(c) *B. nigra* × *B. oleracea* (d) *B.oleracea* × *B. nigra*

Answers 118 (b) 119 (d) 120 (a)

Combined Competitive (Preliminary) Examination, 2010

1. Indian Agriculture is predominantly of
   (a) Subsistence type (b) Commercial type
   (c) Conventional type (d) Highly intensive type
2. Soil Science began with the theory of humus in
   (a) 1654 (b) 1809
   (c) 1906 (d) 1960
3. First field experiment started in
   (a) Rothamsted Experiment Station, England
   (b) PAU, Ludhiana
   (c) TNAU, Coimbatore
   (d) GBPUAT, Pant Nagar
4. The contribution of Agriculture to Indian GDP is
   (a) 20.2% (b) 25.5%
   (c) 18.5% (d) 21.3%
5. The number of Agro Ecological Regions in India for resource planning at National level
   (a) 15 (b) 20
   (c) 25 (d) 30
6. The stable food crop of Southern India is
   (a) Wheat (b) Bajra
   (c) Jowar (d) Rice
7. Rice belongs to the family
   (a) Leguminaceae (b) Poaceae
   (c) Malvaceae (d) Solanaceae

8. The botanical name of Oats is

(a) *Oryza sativa* (b) *Avena sativa*

(c) *Secale cerale* (d) *Hordium vulgare*

9. Repetitive growing of the same crop in the same land is called

(a) Intercropping (b) Sequential Cropping

(c) Multiple Cropping (d) Monocroping

Answers 1 (a) 2 (b) 3 (a) 4 (c) 5 (b) 6 (d) 7 (b) 8 (b) 9 (d)

10. Photo synthetically Active Radiation falls between

(a) 200 – 250 μm (b) 300 – 400 μm

(c) 400 – 700 μm (d) > 700 μm

11. An alternate crop for sugar industry

(a) Beet root (b) Sugar beet

(c) Sweet sorghum (d) Sweet potato

12. Kalyan sona is a variety of

(a) Wheat (b) Rye

(c) Barley (d) Oat

13. Dr. N.E. Borlaugh was responsible for

(a) Watershed Development (b) Green Revolution

(c) White Revolution (d) Integrated Farming System

14. Sweet Corn is botanically called as

(a) *Zea mays tunicata* (b) *Zea mays amylacea*

(c) *Zea mays certain* (d) *Zea mays saccharata*

15. The following is called as "Camel of Crop"

(a) Sorghum (b) Bajra

(c) Maize (d) Rainfed rice

16. The fibre from the following crop is termed as "Fabric of the Future"

(a) Cotton (b) Jute

(c) Agave (d) Hemp

17. The inherent capacity of the soil to supply plant nutrient is

(a) Soil Productivity (b) Soil Fertility

(c) Soil Profile (d) Soil Environment

18. The soil particles ranging from 0.02 – 0.002 mm in size is called as
   (a) Coarse Sand (b) Fine Sand
   (c) Silt (d) Clay

Answers 10 (c) 11 (a) 12 (a) 13 (b) 14 (d) 15 (a) 16 (d) 17 (b) 18 (c)

19. The organic acid produced during the decomposition of organic compounds
   (a) Humic Acid (b) Sulphuric Acid
   (c) Nitric Acid (d) Hydro Chloric Acid

20. Manuring increases the following composition of the soil air
   (a) Nitrogen (b) Oxygen
   (c) Carbon dioxide (d) All the above

21. The diameter of soil micropores ranges between
   (a) 20 – 40 μm (b) 40 – 60 μm
   (c) 60 – 80 μm (d) 02 – 20 μm

22. The following is a microflora responsible for the soil biological environment
   (a) Bacteria (b) Moles
   (c) Protozoa (d) Nematodes

23. Conversion of amino acids to ammonium is called as
   (a) Aminification (b) Ammonification
   (c) Nitrification (d) Hydrolysis

24. The redox Potential of the soil is denoted as
   (a) % (b) Bars
   (c) Eh (d) dSm

25. The criteria for essentiality of elements is given by
   (a) N.E. Borlaugh (b) Buckman and Brady
   (c) Black (d) Arnon

26. The nutrient required for the synthesis of ATP
   (a) N (b P
   (c) K (d) Zn

27. Calcium nutrient is most needed for
   (a) Rice (b) Maize
   (c) Groundnut (d) Sunflower

Answers 19 (a) 20 (d) 21 (d) 22 (a) 23 (b)24 (c)25 (d) 26 (b) 27 (b)

28. The nutrient responsible for the formation of chlorophyll

(a) Fe (b) Zn
(c) Mn (d) Mg

29. The following is used for the preparation of enriched farm yard manure

(a) Super phosphate (b) Urea
(c) Gypsum (d) Ferrous sulphate

30. Which one of the following is green leaf manure?

(a) *Sesbania aculeata* (b) *Glyricidia maculeata*
(c) *Crotalaria juncea* (d) *Sesbania speciosa*

31. *Karanj* is a common name of

(a) *Pongamia glabra* (b) *Azadirachta indica*
(c) *Calotrpis gigantean* (d) *Tephrosia purpurea*

32. The nutrient content of Zinc Sulphate is

(a) 36% (b) 42%
(c) 21% (d) 16%

33. The available Nitrogen in oil is estimated by

(a) Walkley and Black Method (b) Olsen's method
(c) Ammonium Acetate Method (d) Alkaline Permanganate Method

34. The major fertiliser marketed in India

(a) DAP (b) SSP
(c) KCL (d) Urea

35. A material used as soil amendment

(a) Lime (b) Urea
(c) Fish meal (d) Karanj cake

36. Photosynthesis can be studied under the process of

(a) Entry of carbon dioxide (b) Photolysis
(c) Carbon dioxide reduction (d) All the above

Answers 28 (d) 29 (b) 30 (b) 31 (a) 32 (c)33 (b)34 (d) 35 (a) 36 (d)

37. The following is a C4 plant

(a) Rice (b) Maize
(c) Cotton (d) Sunflower

38. The carrier concept theory of plant nutrition was formulated by
   (a) Olsen (b) Brey
   (c) Van den Honert (d) Donnen

39. Vesicular Arbuscular Mycorrhiza (VAM) is commonly applied for
   (a) Perennials (b) Annuals
   (c) Biennials (d) Hydrophonics

40. A biofertilser which can be used as dual crop is
   (a) Green manure (b) Azolla
   (c) VAM (d) Rhizhobium

41. The following is a slow release Nitrogenous fertiliser
   (a) CAN (b) Urea
   (c) Ureaform (d) Anhydrous Ammonia

42. Intervienal chlorosis in leaves is caused by the deficiency of
   (a) Nitrogen (b) Iron
   (c) Zinc (d) Magnesium

43. Which of the following induces leaf and fruit abscission?
   (a) NAA (b) CCC
   (c) IBA (d) ABA

44. The following is an auxin and used as herbicide at higher doses
   (a) 2, 4 – D (b) GA
   (c) NAA (d) IBA

45.Emasculation is done to devoid
   (a) Flowers (b) Pollen
   (c) Gynaecium (d) Fruits

Answers 37 (b) 38 (c) 39 (a) 40 (a) 41 (a) 42 (b) 43 (d) 44 (a) 45 (b)

46. A commonly found parasitic weed of sugarcane
   (a) *Orabanche* sp (b) *Cuscuta* sp
   (c) *Striga* sp (d) *Loranthus* sp

47. Efficiency and effectiveness of conventional breeding can be improved by
   (a) Selection (b) Mutation
   (c) CMS (d) Molecular Markers

48. Important hybrid of maize
   (a) Vijay (b) Hi Starch
   (c) Sona (d) CO 5

49. Father of Hybrid Rice
    (a) Prof. Yuvan Long Ping (b) Dr. N. E. Borlaugh
    (c) Dr. M. S. Swaminathan (d) Dr. G. S. Kush

50. Golden rice is enriched with
    (a) Vitamin B1 (b) Vitamin D
    (c) Vitamin C (d) Vitamin A

51. Major type of wheat cultivated in India
    (a) *Triticum diurum* (b) *Triticum aestivum*
    (c) *Triticum sphaerococum* (d) All the above

52. Protein content in pulses ranging from
    (a) 10 – 15% (b) 15 – 20%
    (c) 20 – 25% (d) 25 – 30%

53. A value added product of Soybean
    (a) Macroni (b) Candy
    (c) Butter (d) Tofu

54. An edible oil with rich of linoleic fatty acid
    (a) Sunflower oil (b) Ground nut oil
    (c) Gingelly oil (d) Coconut oil

Answers 46 (c) 47 (a) 48 (b) 49 (a) 50 (d)51 (b) 52 (c) 3 (d) 54 (a)

55. Phenyl Mercuric Acetate (PMA) has following action as ntitranspirant
    (a) Film forming (b) Stomatal closing
    (c) Reflectance (d) Growth retardant

56. Which weed is classified as sedge
    (a) *Panicum repens* (b) *Cyperus rotundus*
    (c) *Digeria arvensis* (d) *Chloris barbata*

57. The safe grain moisture content for storage of rice
    (a) 14% (b) 16%
    (c) 18% (d) 20%

58. When the growth is complete and photosynthates are no longer translocated, it is called
    (a) Senescence (b) Maturity
    (c) Physiological maturity (d) Harvest maturity

59. Loss of nutrients beyond root zone along with water is called

(a) Translocation (b) Immobilisation

(c) Runoff (d) Leaching

60. Thermopile organisms thrive at a temperature of

(a) > 40^0C (b) 20 – 30^0C

(c) 10 – 20^0C (d) < 10^0C

61. Cardinal temperature denotes

(a) Maximum temperature (b) Minimum temperature

(c) Optimum temperature (d) All the above

62. Assmann psychrometer is used for observing

(a) Relative humidity (b) Sunshine

(c) Maximum temperature (d) Minimum temperature

63. The botanical name of Apple

(a) *Malus sylvestris* (b) *Pyrus communis*

(c) *Prunus salicina* (d) *Ananas sativus*

Answers 55 (b) 56 (c) 57 (a) 58 (a) 59 (d) 60 (a) 61 (d) 62 (a) 63 (a)

64. Which one is a non edible oil cake?

(a) Coconut (b) Ground nut

(c) Castor (d) Sesame

65. Which of the crop is self pollinated?

(a) Millets (b) Onion

(c) Rice (d) Cotton

66. Foundation seed is obtained from

(a) Nucleus seed (b) Breeder seed

(c) Registered seed (d) Certified seed

67. The following is used in biological measure of soil conservation

(a) Neem (b) Agave

(c) Casuarina (d) Glyricidia

68. *Cucumis sativus* is the botanical name of

(a) *Ashgourd* (b) *Bottlegourd*

(c) *Cucumber* (d) *Sweet pepper*

69. Karimunda is a variety of
    (a) Pepper (b) Ginger
    (c) Turmeric (d) Onion

70. The ecosystem of the following State favours cultivation of spices
    (a) Jammu & Kashmir (b) Maharashtra
    (c) Assam (d) Kerala

71. A commonly used chemical for rhizome rot
    (a) Carbofuran (b) Bordeaux Mixture
    (c) Mancozeb (d) Dimethoate

72. Which of the following is used as standard for Vanilla?
    (a) Coconut (b) Arecaunut
    (c) Cocoa (d) Glyricidia

Answers 64(c) 65 (c) 66 (b) 67 (b) 68 (c) 69 (a) 70 (d) 71 (c) 72 (c)

73. Skiffing is a pruning method followed in
    (a) Tea (b) Coffee
    (c) Rubber (d) Cocoa

74. The annual yield of rubber in South India is
    (a) 500 kg/ha (b) 375 kg/ha
    (c) 750 kg/ha (d) 1000 kg/ha

75. *Cymbopogon winterianus* is the botanical name of
    (a) Citronella (b) Lemon grass
    (c) Palmarosa (d) Patcholi

76. Following is an export variety of Mango
    (a) Neelam (b) Bangalora
    (c) Alphonsa (d) Mulgoa

77. Papaya seeds are viable upto
    (a) 1 – 2 months (b) 3 – 4 months
    (c) One year (d) > one year

78. Number of trees accommodated in one acre of land with a spacing of 20 × 20 ft
    (a) 72 trees (b) 89 trees
    (c) 109 trees (d) 132 trees

79. Chlorotic symptom beginning in older leaves because of the deficiency of

(a) Nitrogen (b) Phosphorous
(c) Iron (d) Manganese

80. Irish Peach is a variety of

(a) Mango (b) Apple
(c) Pear (d) Plum

81. Scurvy can be prevented by intake of

(a) Vitamin A (b) Vitamin B1
(c) Vitamin C (d) Vitamin D

Answers 73 (a) 74 (b) 75 (b) 76 (c) 77 (b) 78 (c) 79 (a) 80 (b) 81 (c)

82. Post harvest losses in fruits and vegetables account to

(a) 5 – 10% (b) 10 – 30%
(c) > 30% (d) < 5%

83. Brown Plant Hopper is a pest of

(a) Sorghum (b) Wheat
(c) Rice (d) Maize

84. *Pseudomonas fluorescens* is used in

(a) INM (b) IWM
(c) IPM (d) SSNM

85. *Chilo infuscatellus* in sugarcane is commonly called as

(a) Shoot borer (b) Internode borer
(c) Top shoot borer (d) White grub

86. Woolly aphid (*Ceratovacuna lanigera*) is a common pest found in

(a) Apple (b) Sugarcane
(c) Mango (d) Tomato

87. Acid delinting in cotton is done by

(a) Conc. Sulphuric Acid (b) Conc. Nitric Acid
(c) Conc. Hydrochloric acid (d) Combination of all above

88. Soil application of carbofuran 3G in cotton controls

(a) Whitefly (b) Mites
(c) Cutworms (d) Stem weevil

89. *Rotylenchulus reniformis* is

(a) Lesion nematode (b) Lance nematode
(c) Reniform nematode (d) Rootknot nematode

90. Application of the following is done in biocontrol of plant pests and diseases

(a) *Rhizoctonia bataticola* (b) *Pseudomonas fluorescens*

(c) *Pempherulus affinis* (d) *Bemisia tabaci*

Answers 82 (b) 83 (c) 84 (c) 85 (a) 86 (a) 87 (a) 88 (c) 89 (d) 90 (b)

91. *Trichogramma chilonis* is called as

(a) Larval parasite (b) Pupal parasite

(c) Adult parasite (d) Egg parasite

92. Which of the following is used in the control of pests?

(a) Inter cropping (b) Mixed cropping

(c) Trap cropping (d) Multiple cropping

93. The accurate quantification of pesticide residues is determined by

(a) GC (b) HPLC

(c) TLC (d) GLC

94. The water used for one ha in Ultra low volume sprayer is

(a) 2 – 3 litres (b) 3 – 4 litres

(c) 4 – 5 litres (d) < one litre

95. Uniform distribution of spray fluid is determined by

(a) Nozzle (b) Pumps

(c) Tanks (d) Pressure

96. Which sprayer is used for spraying on tall trees like coconut?

(a) Knapsack sprayer (b) Power sprayer

(c) Rocker sprayer (d) Boom sprayer

97. Poultry management in farm is

(a) Competitive enterprise (b) Complementary enterprise

(c) Supplementary enterprise (d) Individual enterprise

98. Enterprise budgeting is used to define

(a) Total Income (b) Total Expenditure

(c) Returns above defined costs (d) Benefit Cost ratio

99. The cost of using a resource in one way is the return that could be earned from using that resource in its next best, most profitable alternative use is

(a) Fixed cost (b) Opportunity cost

(c) Variable cost (d) Total cost

Answers 91 (d) 92 (c) 93 (b) 94 (d) 95 (a) 96 (c) 97 (c) 98 (c) 99 (b)

100. The costs vary according to the size of the enterprise and the amount of inputs used
   (a) Total cost (b) Fixed cost
   (c) Variable cost (d) Opportunity cost

101. The value lost by an item over its useful life
   (a) Depreciation (b) Loss
   (c) Variable cost (d) Cash flow

102. A method of making a comparative study of the cost-and-return analysis resulting from a change in a part of the business organisation is
   (a) Enterprise budgeting (b) Partial budgeting
   (c) Total budgeting (d) Farm planning

103. The National Centre for Agricultural Economics and Policy Research (NCAP) is situated at
   (a) New Delhi (b) Hyderabad
   (c) Bangalore (d) Mumbai

104. Night blindness disease is associated with the deficiency of
   (a) Vitamin A (b) Vitamin B
   (c) Vitamin C (d) Vitamin D

105. Lycopene is present in
   (a) Sweet potato (b) Tomato
   (c) Black berry (d) Rasp berry

106. A length of growing period (LGP) supports double cropping is
   (a) > 210 days (b) 90 – 150 days
   (c) < 90 days (d) 150 – 210 days

107. An Agro Organization and Professional Society at the International Level
   (a) Fertilizer Association of India (FAI)
   (b) International Food Policy Research Institute (IFPRI)
   (c) Agricultural Technology Marketing Agency (ATMA)
   (d) Agriculture and Processed Food Products Export Development Authority

108. India is the largest producer of
   (a) Rice (b) Coconut
   (c) Wheat (d) Sugar

Answers 100 (c) 101 (a) 102 (b) 103 (a) 104 (a) 105 (b) 106 (b) 107 (d) 108 (b)

109. Bt seeds are popular in
   (a) Cotton (b) Vegetables
   (c) Rice (d) Maize

110. National Agricultural Extension Project (NAEP) was supported by
   (a) NABARD (b) World Bank
   (c) FAO (d) ICRISAT

111. Establishment of "Ryot Samparka Kendras" or "Farmers' Contact Centres" was initiated by government of
   (a) Karnataka (b) Maharashtra
   (c) Kerala (d) Tamil Nadu

112. e-Choupal is an extension system by
   (a) ITC (b) Coffee Board
   (c) Tea Board (d) Spices Board

113. Which of the following is considered as Public Extension?
   (a) Extension by NGO (b) Extension by State Departments
   (c) Extension by private institution (d) Extension by Mass media

114. Community Development Programme in India was inaugurated in
   (a) 1952 (b) 1957
   (c) 1947 (d) 1950

115. The Intensive Agricultural District Programme, launched in five districts by the central government in
   (a) 1960 (b) 1958
   (c) 1962 (d) 1957

116. A water intensive crop
   (a) Cotton (b) Sugarcane
   (c) Maize (d) Sorghum

117. Nipping is a practice in
   (a) Sugarcane (b) Cotton
   (c) Tobacco (d) Forage crops

Answers 109 (a) 110 (b) 111(a) 112 (a) 113 (b) 114 (a) 115 (a) 116 (b) 117 (b)

118. Rice prefers Nitrogen in the form of
   (a) Nitrate (b) Amide
   (c) Ammoniacal (d) Nitrous

119. Decomposition of organic matter in rice soils generate

(a) Ethane (b) Methane

(c) Propane (d) Butane

120. Which of the following location of tea has more of export potential?

(a) Darjeeling (b) Coorg

(c) Nilgiris (d) Munnar

Answers 118 (c) 119 (b) 120 (a)

State Public Service Commission (Raao, Agriculture Assistant Officer-2013)

1. Blue revolution refers to
   (a) Poultry (b) Agriculture
   (c) Food Processing (d) Fisheries
2. Area under dry land agriculture in India is
   (a) 70% (b) 60%
   (c) 50% (d) 40%
3. First man made cereal is
   (a) Wheat (b) Triticale
   (c) Rice (d) Bajra
4. The cotton developed by transfer of Bt gene in cotton plant is known as
   (a) Organic Cotton (b) Inorganic Cotton
   (c) Transgenic Cotton (d) Non-transgenic Cotton
5. Yellow revolution is associated with
   (a) Milk (b) Pulses
   (c) Cereals (d) Oil Seeds
6. The most deficient micro-nutrient in India soil is
   (a) Zn (b) Fe
   (c) Mn (d) N_2
7. 'Striga' is associated with crop
   (a) Wheat (b) Pulses
   (c) Sorghum (d) Mango
8. 'Pusa Bold' is a variety of
   (a) Wheat (b) Mustard
   (c) Gram (d) Groundnut

9. Support price for agricultural commodities are announced by
   (a) Indian Council of Agricultural Research (ICAR)
   (b) Agricultural Price Commission
   (c) Department of Agriculture Research & Education (DARE)
   (d) Food & Agricultural Organization (FAO)

Answers 1 (d) 2 (a) 3 (b) 4 (c) 5 (d) 6 (a) 7 (c) 8 (b) 9 (b)

10. Which of the following is not a farming system on the basis of land use and cultural practices classification?
   (a) Specialized farming (b) Tenant farming
   (c) Mixed farming (d) Diversified farming

11. When two single crosses are crossed, the resulting hybrid is known as
   (a) Double Cross (b) Top Cross
   (c) Three way Cross (d) Double Top Cross

12. Hybrid varieties were first commercially exploited in
   (a) Bajra (b) Maize
   (c) Sorghum (d) Cotton

13. The plant part to be cultured in vitro is known as
   (a) Zygotic plant (b) Miniature plant
   (c) Explant (d) Infant plant

14. The initial seed of a variety produced by the breeder is known as
   (a) Breeder's seed (b) Nucleus seed
   (c) Certified seed (d) Registered seed

15. Certified seed is produced from
   (a) Breeder's seed (b) Nucleus seed
   (c) Registered seed (d) Foundation seed

16. The progeny of a self pollinated plant is
   (a) Homozygous (b) Heterozygous
   (c) Heterogeneous (d) Heterozygous & Heterogeneous

17. The term heterosis was first used by
   (a) Punnet (b) Bateson
   (c) Mandel (d) Shull

18. Development of fruit without fertilization is called
(a) Parthenogenesis (b) Parthenocarpy
(c) Apomixis (d) Budding

Answers 10 (b) 11 (a) 12 (b) 13 (c) 14 (b) 15 (c) 16 (a) 17 (d) 18 (b)

19. The sugar present in DNA is called
(a) Ribose (b) Deoxyribose
(c) Maltose (d) Fructose

20. When single gene is affecting more than one character, it is known as
(a) Pleiotropy (b) Penetrance
(c) Polymorphism (d) Phenocopy

21. Ganga 5 is a hybrid of
(a) Sorghum (b) Wheat
(c) Cotton (d) Maize

22. A character governed by one gene is called
(a) Polygenic (b) Monogenic
(c) Digenic (d) Trigenic

23. The oxidized zone of puddle paddy is having a thickness of
(a) Top 1 – 10 mm (b) Top 45 mm
(c) Top 25 mm (d) Top 15 – 20 mm

24. The area required for DAPOG nursery for sowing 1 hectare rice is
(a) 50 m^2 (b) 30 m^2
(c) 100 m^2 (d) 10 m^2

25. The seed rate (kg/ha) of hybrid rice is
(a) 25 kg/ha (b) 5 k/ha
(c) 45 kg/h (d) 15 kg/ha

26. Simplest and common method of sugarcane planting is
(a) Trench method (b) Ridge & furrow method
(c) Planting in flat beds (d) Rayungans method

27. Best suited soils for ground nut cultivation is
(a) Sandy (b) Sandy loam
(c) Clay loam (d) Sandy and clay loam

Answers 19 (b) 20 (a) 21 (d) 22 (b) 23 (a) 24 (c) 25 (d) 26 (b) 27 (b)

28. The sowing depth of dwarf wheat varieties is

(a) 6 -7 cm (b) 2 – 3 cm

(c) 4 – 5 cm (d) 5 – 6 cm

29. Which crop is considered as major oil seed crop in India?

(a) Groundnut (b) Sesame

(c) Castor (d) Rage seed & mustard

30. Most commonly used herbicide to kill broad leaf weeds in wheat field is

(a) Alachlor (b) Atrazin

(c) 2-4-D (d) Isoproturon

31. Gypsum application required for the development of better pods in groundnut is

(a) 250 kg/ha (b) 800 kg/ha

(c) 500 kg/ha (d) 1000 kg/ha

32. The pop in groundnut is due to deficiency of

(a) Ca (b) N

(c) P (d) K

33. Most commonly and widely cultivated pulse crop in India is

(a) Redgram (b) Pea

(c) Lentil (d) Chickpea

34. For kabuli gram inter row spacing is

(a) 30 cm (b) 75 cm

(c) 45 cm (d) 90 cm

35. Major pest of gram is

(a) Pod borer (b) White grub

(c) Cut worm (d) Stem borer

36. The highest production of mustard is contributed by the state

(a) Gujarat (b) Rajasthan

(c) Uttar Pradesh (d) Madhya Pradesh

Answers 28 (d) 29 (a) 30 (c) 31 (a) 32 (a) 33 (a) 34 (a) 35 (a) 36 (b)

37. The sprinkler system of irrigation is most suitable for

(a) Undulated soils (b) Saline soils

(c) Clay soils (d) Acidic soils

38. In Rajasthan highest area of crop in kharif season is covered under
(a) Cotton (b) Maize
(c) Bajra (d) Sorghum

39. The crop which is used both as pulses and oil seed crop
(a) Soyabean (b) Blackgarm
(c) Cowpea (d) Arhar

40. In Rajasthan most common mixed cropping is
(a) Gram + Mustard (b) Mustard + Wheat
(c) Mustard + Barley (d) Groundnut + Til

41. The best green manuring crop is
(a) Guar (b) Sunhemp
(c) Dhaincha (d) Berseem

42. The injury caused by the relatively low temperature above the freezing point is called
(a) Freezing injury (b) Mechanical injury
(c) Dehydration injury (d) Chilling injury

43. Inherent capacity of soil to supply nutrients in balanced form is called
(a) Soil productivity (b) Soil fertility
(c) Fertility index (d) Productivity index

44. Well rotted FYM contain N
(a) 0.5% (b) 1.0%
(c) 1.5% (d) 2.0%

45. 'Mg' and 'S' are termed as
(a) Primary nutrients (b) Micronutrients
(c) Ultra-micronutrient (d) Secondary nutrients

Answers 37 (a) 38 (d) 39 (a) 40 (d) 41 (b) 42 (d) 43 (b) 44 (a) 45 (d)

46. Chlorosis refers to
(a) Burning of leaf tissue (b) Yellowing of leaf tissue
(c) Death of leaf tissue (d) Development of reddish brown colour on leaf

47. Which of the soil has higher buffering capacity?
(a) Sandy soils (b) Clayey soils
(c) Loamy sand soils (d) Loamy soils

48. Under high source irrigation water we will prefer to grow
    (a) Barley (b) Gram
    (c) Pea (d) Wheat

49. Khaira disease of rice is due to deficiency of
    (a) Zinc (b) Iron
    (c) Nitrogen (d) Calcium

50. Very important constituent in fruits for preparing jelly is
    (a) Sugar (b) Vitamin
    (c) Pectin (d) Cellulose

51. Maximum number of fruit plants can be planted in the orchard by the system
    (a) Triangular system (b) Hexagonal system
    (c) Rectangular system (d) Square system

52. Which flower can be grown in all season?
    (a) Marigold (b) Corn flower
    (c) Chrysanthemum (d) Candituft

53. Which of the following is the fruit vegetable?
    (a) Potato (b) Sweet potato
    (c) Tomato (d) Spinach

54. Which is not a growth promoter?
    (a) Cytokinins (b) Abscissic acid
    (c) Auxins (d) Gibberellins

Answers 46 (b) 47 (b) 48 (c) 49 (a) 50 (a)51 (b)52 (a) 53 (c) 54 (b)

55. Which is not fruit of arid climatic conditions?
    (a) Date palm (b) Banana
    (c) Pomegranate (d) Ber

56. Date palm should be propagated by
    (a) Seeds (b) Rhizomes
    (c) Buddings (d) Suckers (Offshoots)

57. Most economic method of irrigation of orchard under water scarcity condition is
    (a) Drip system (b) Sprinkler system
    (c) Flood system (d) Ring system

58. Seedlessness in grapes is due to
(a) Parthenocarpy (b) Embryo abortion
(c) Polyploidy (d) Lack of pollination

59. Snowball 16 is a variety of
(a) Cauliflower (b) Cabbage
(c) Potato (d) Tomato

60. The main host tree for the cultivation of lac insect is
(a) Palas (b) Khejri
(c) Babul (d) Pipal

61. Loose smut of wheat is a disease
(a) Internally seed borne (b) Air borne
(c) Soil borne (d) Externally seed borne

62. Powdery mildew disease is caused by
(a) Virus (b) Bacterium
(c) Nematode (d) Fungus

63. Primary source of infection to green ear disease of Bajra is
(a) Seed & Soil (b) Air
(c) Insect (d) Soil

Answers 55 (b) 56 (d) 57 (a) 58 (b) 59 (a) 60 (a) 61 (a) 62 (d) 63 (a)

64. Tomato leaf curl is caused by
(a) Virus (b) Bacteria
(c) Fungus (d) Mycoplasma

65. Most effective fungicide against powdery mildew disease is
(a) Capstan (b) Dithane Z-78
(c) Bavistin (d) Karathane

66. Which one of the following is not a physical factor affecting the type of farming?
(a) Topography (b) Climate
(c) Labour supply (d) Soil

67. Which one of the following is not component of farm business?
(a) Capital (b) Environment
(c) Land (d) Management

68. Cost calculated per quintal is known as
    (a) Cost of farming (b) Cost of cultivation
    (c) Cost of production (d) Total cost

69. The Krishi Vigyan Kendra's (KVK's) are 100% funded by
    (a) State Government
    (b) Indian Council of Agriculture Research (ICAR)
    (c) University Grant Commission (UGC)
    (d) Council of Scientific & Industrial Research (CSIR)

70. The effective extension method to improves farmers about a particular recommended practice for a specific area is
    (a) Television (b) Radio
    (c) Demonstration (d) Pamphlates

71. Which of the following is not a method of group communication?
    (a) Conference (b) National Demonstration
    (c) Farm & home visits (d) Field trips

72. Damping off disease of seedling is mainly caused by the species of
    (a) Mucor (b) Puccinia
    (c) Pythium (d) Ustilago

Answers 64 (a) 65 (d) 66 (c) 67 (b) 68 (c) 69 (b) 70 (c) 71 (c) 72 (c)

73. Late blight of potato is caused is caused by
    (a) Phytophthora infestans (b) Sclerospora graminis
    (c) Alternaria solani (d) Coletotrichum falcatum

74. Root knot disease of brinjal is caused by
    (a) Fungi (b) Bacteria
    (c) Nematode (d) Viruses

75. Which of the following elements is a micronutrient?
    (a) Boron (b) Nitrogen
    (c) Phosphorous (d) Magnesium

76. Movement of water molecular from a solution with their higher concentration towards their lower concentration solution through a semi-permeable membrane is known as
    (a) Diffusion (b) Osmosis
    (c) Imbibition (d) Transpiration

77. Which one of the following plants is an example of incomplete dominance?

(a) Pisum sativum (b) Lathyrus odoratus

(c) Raphanus sativus (d) Mirabilis jalapa

78. Soil particle size of silt soil ranges between

(a) 2.0 mm to 0.2 mm (b) 02 mm to 0.02 mm

(c) 0.02 mm to 0.002 mm (d) 0.002 mm to 0.0002 mm

79. pH of saline soils is

(a) 8.5 (b) 9.5

(c) 10.5 (d) 11.5

80. Sodic soils can be made more productive by adding

(a) Boron (b) Calcium

(c) Phosphorus (d) Sodium

81. Which one of following is commonly used for naval disinfection?

(a) Distilled water (b) Tincture of Iodine

(c) Sodium chloride (d) Iodex

Answers 73 (a) 74 (c) 75 (a) 76 (b) 77 (d) 78 (c) 79 (a) 80 (b) 81 (b)

82. First milk after the parturition of cow is called

(a) Toned milk (b) Butter milk

(c) Colostrum (d) Cheese

83. Which one of the following is a disease of young calf

(a) Thiloreosis (b) Mastitis

(c) Acidosis (d) Osteoporosis

84. The full form IVLF is

(a) Institution village livestock project

(b) International value linked plan

(c) Institutional village livelihood development plan

(d) Institution village linkage program

85. Which one of the following is a training institute?

(a) ATMA (b) KVK

(c) DRDA (d) ATIC

86. Foot and Mouth disease is caused by

(a) Fungal (b) Bacterial

(c) Viral (d) Parasitic

87. The inflammation of udder is known as
    (a) Matritis (b) Mastitis
    (c) Ootitis (d) Gastritis

88. Heifer becomes breedable at approximate age of
    (a) 1-2 year (b) 4-5 year
    (c) 2-3 year (d) Above 5 year

89. Recommended bred of buffalo for Ajmer district is
    (a) Murrah (b) Surti
    (c) Jafrabati (d) Nili Ravi

90. Which one of following is a milky breed of cattle?
    (a) Haryanvi (b) Nagori
    (c) Sahiwal (d) Mcvati

Answers 82 (c) 83 (a) 84 (d) 85 (a) 86 (c)87 (b)88 (a) 89 (a) 90 (c)

91. Gir breed of cattle is appropriate for
    (a) Ajmer area (b) Jaisalmer area
    (c) Bikaner area (d) Jalore area

92. Milk production potential of good breed of 'Gir' cattle is
    (a) 1000-2000 litre (b) 2000-2500 litre
    (c) 2500-4500 litre (d) 5000-8000 litre

93. Best time for doing A-I, after the start of heat in cow is
    (a) After 8-10 hrs (b) After 12-18 hrs
    (c) After 24-30 hrs (d) After 30-36 hrs

94. Which one of following gas is used for storage of semen?
    (a) Oxygen (b) Carbon dioxide
    (c) Nitrogen (d) Argan

95. Which one of following disease can be transmitted through bulls in natural breeding?
    (a) Brucillosis (b) Parakeratosis
    (c) Silicosis (d) Mastitis

96. "Silage making' is a method of
    (a) Preservation of fodder in green stage (b) Preservation of pulse crops
    (c) Preservation of oil cakes (d) Preservation of cereals

97. 'Hey making' is a method of
(a) Preservation of rice (b) Preservation of wheat
(c) Preservation of fodder (d) Preservation of pulses

98. 'Pica' disease is caused by deficiency of
(a) Vitamins (b) Minerals
(c) Protein (d) Crude fibre

99. Osteoporosis disease is associated with
(a) Ca (b) P
(c) Mg (d) Sulphur

Answers 91 (a) 92 (a) 93 (b) 94 (c) 95 (a) 96 (a) 97 (c) 98 (b) 99 (a)

100. 'Grassy Titeny' disease is caused by
(a) Deficiency of Mg (b) Deficiency of Sulphur
(c) Excess of Ca (d) Excess of crude fibre

101. For feeding of livestock groundnut cake is a good source of
(a) Minerals (b) Vitamins
(c) Proteins (d) Fat

102. Quality of dry fodder can be improved by treatment of
(a) Common salt (b) Urea
(c) Potassium permagnate (d) DAP

103. First compartment of stomach of ruminant is called
(a) Omesum (b) Abomesum
(c) Reticulum (d) Rumen

104. In a balanced ratio for buffalo
(a) 2/3 part comes from roughage 1/3 from concentrate
(b) 1/3 part comes from roughage 2/3 from concentrate
(c) 1/2 part comes from roughage 1/2 from concentrate
(d) 1/4 part comes from roughage 3/4 from concentrate

105. Azolla is a
(a) Algae (b) Fern
(c) Tree (d) Fruit

106. ________ is a draught breed of cattle
(a) Sahiwal (b) Nagori
(c) Red Sindhi (d) Jersey

107. Average gestation period of buffalo is

(a) 407 days (b) 307 days

(c) 270 days (d) 330 days

108. Endocrine glands secrets

(a) Enzymes (b) Co-enzyme

(c) Hormones (d) Sweat

Answers 100 (a) 101 (c) 102 (b) 103 (d) 104 (a) 105 (b) 106 (b) 107(b 108 (c)

109. Night blindness is associated with

(a) Vitamin C (b) Vitamin A

(c) Vitamin K (d) Vitamin B-Complex

110. Scurvy is associated with

(a) Vitamin C (b) Vitamin B Complex

(c) Vitamin D (d) Vitamin E

111. Dehorning in calf can be done by use of

(a) Sodium chloride (b) Caustic Soda

(c) Alum (d) Sodium bicarbonate

112. National dairy Development Board is situated in __________ state

(a) Rajasthan (b) Gujarat

(c) Punjab (d) Haryana

113. Head office of Indian Council of Agriculture (ICAR) is situated at

(a) Pune (b) Bangalore

(c) Hyderabad (d) New Delhi

114. Black quarter is a disease of

(a) Camel (b) Horse

(c) Cattle (d) Dog

115. Surra is a common disease of

(a) Pig (b) Poultry

(c) Camel (d) Dog

116. Vermicompost is made by use of

(a) Earthworms (b) House fly

(c) Termites (d) Birds

117. Ticks infestation in animals may be controlled by use of

(a) Melathion (b) Lime

(c) Chalk powder (d) Common salt

Answers 109 (b) 110 (a) 111(b) 112(b) 113(d) 114 (c) 115 (c) 116 (a) 117 (a)

118. Which country produces highest milk in the world?

(a) U.S. of America (b) China

(c) Denmark (d) India

119. Reproduction in animals is associated with deficiency of

(a) Vitamin E (b) Ca

(c) P (d) Mg

120. Sirohi is a breed of

(a) Goat (b) Horse

(c) Sheep (d) Camel

Answers 118 (d) 119 (c) 120 (a)

State Public Service Commission (HCSEX Agriculture Prelims-2014)

1. Black soil is used for the cultivation of
   (a) Jute (b) Wheat
   (c) Cotton (d) Sugarcane

2. Common herbicide used in wheat is
   (a) 2,4 –Dichlorophenoxyacetic acid (b) Atrazine
   (c) Isoproturon (d) Pendimethalin

3. Delinting of cotton seed may be done with
   (a) Sulphuric acid (b) Citric acid
   (c) Sodium hydroxide (d) Ammonium chloride

4. Mixed farming is referred only to
   (a) Growing of crops together by mixing the seeds
   (b) Growing of cash crops and food grains together
   (c) Crop production combined with dairy farming at farm
   (d) Growing of fruits and vegetables mixed

5. Name the kharif season fodder crop
   (a) Oats (b) Lucerne
   (c) Sorghurn (d) Berseem

6. Phalaris minor is a weed found with
   (a) Wheat (b) Cowpea
   (c) Barley (d) Oat

7. Arhar (pigeonpea) grows well in which climate
   (a) Tropical and subtropical (b) Temperate
   (c) Humid and temperate (d) Sub-humid and temperate

8. Causal agent of anthracnose disease in sorghum is

(a) *Puccinia purpurea* (b) *Helminthosporium turcicum*

(c) *Colletotrichum graminicola* (d) *Gleourcospora sorghi*

9. Which one of the following is the principal N'fixing algal community of blue-green algae?

(a) Rhizobium (b) Anabaena

(c) Azotobactor (d) Azospirillum

Answers 1 (c) 2 (a) 3 (a) 4 (c) 5 (c) 6 (a) 7 (a) 8 (c) 9 (b)

10. What is impact of excessive application of nitrogenous fertilizer on sugar content in juice of sugarcane?

(a) Decrease (b) Increase

(c) Constant (d) Crystallized

11. Amongst the following which is the food preservative?

(a) Celphos (b) Calcium cynamide

(c) Sodium benzoate (d) Potassium permagnate

12. An apple tree gives the fruits after

(a) 5 years of planting (b) 3 years of planting

(c) 2 years of planting (d) 8 years of planting

13. Botanical name of carnation is

(a) *Celosia cristata* (b) *Tagetis errecta*

(c) *Dianthus caryophyllus* (d) *Centuria cyanus*

14. Muscat red is a variety of

(a) Grapes (b) Pomegranate

(c) Plums (d) Apple

15. Plant bearing male and female flowers is called

(a) Monoecious (b) Monophrodite

(c) Bisexual (d) Hermophrodite

16. Which hormone is found in ripened fruits?

(a) Ethylene (b) Auxin

(c) Gibberellins (d) IAA

17. A vertical section of soil body which shows different layers is known as

(a) Soil horizons (b) Soil profile

(c) Regolith (d) Parent material

18. Active soil forming factors include

(a) Vegetation and topography (b) Time, topography and climate

(c) Time and vegetation (d) Vegetation and climate

Answers 10 (a) 11 (c) 12 (a) 13 (c)14 (a) 15 (a)16 (a) 17 (b) 18 (d)

19. Available phosphorus of less than 10 kg/ha of soil is considered as

(a) Low (b) Medium

(c) High (d) Trace

20. Azotobacter spp. fix atmospheric nitrogen

(a) As symbionts on sugarcane (b) As symbionts on rice

(c) As symbionts on legumes (d) In free soil

21. Wet black soils are

(a) Very hard (b) Very soft

(c) Soft (d) Hard

22. Hydraulic conductivity of soils varies directly with

(a) Capillary porosity (b) Non-capillary porosity

(c) Total porosity (d) Water holding capacity

23. Microbial population of a soil in general

(a) Decreases with depth (b) Increases with depth

(c) Constant throughout the profile(d) No specific trend

24. Mycorrhiza-infected plants show better ability of absorption of the nutrients, especially

(a) Iron (b) Manganese

(c) Potassium (d) Phosphorus

25. Occurrence of quartz in high amounts makes a rock

(a) Hard (b) Soft

(c) Alkaline (d) Acidic

26. Red soils are found maximum in

(a) Uttar Pradesh (b) Madhya Pradesh

(c) Assam (d) Tamil Nadu

27. Saline soils are reclaimed/managed by

(a) Addition of gypsum (b) Addition of lime

(c) Leaching the soluble salts (d) Addition of pyrite

Answers 19 (a) 20 (d) 21 (b) 22 (c) 23 (a) 24 (c) 25 (a) 26 (d) 27 (b)

28. The global average of solar radiation reaching the earth is
    (a) 20% (b) 30%
    (c) 40% (d) 50%

29. Arachnids and insects contain malpighian tubules as organ of
    (a) Respiration (b) Excretion
    (c) Digestion (d) Secretion

30. Classification of phylum mollusca is based on
    (a) Locomotory organs (b) Respiratory organs
    (c) Digestive organs (d) Reproductive organs

31. *Diacrisia obliqua* is the scientific name of
    (a) Termite (b) Top borer
    (c) Bihar hairy caterpillar (d) Leaf hoper

32. Fore-gut of insects is lined internally by
    (a) Peritrophic membrane (b) Epithelial membrane
    (c) Cuticular intima (d) Taenidia

33. Texture of the soil can be changed by
    (a) Use of fertilizers (b) Use of tillage practices
    (c) Use of manures (d) None of these

34. *Dasineura lini* is pest of
    (a) Castor (c) Seasamum
    (b) Linseed (d) Groundnut

35. Insects feeding on plants of several genera within a family are called
    (a) Phytophagous (b) Polyphagous
    (c) Oligophagous (d) Monophagous

36. Most of the insects cannot survive the temperatures above
    (a) 29.9^{0}C (b) 39.9^{0}C
    (c) 49.9^{0}C (d) 59.9^{0}C

Answers 28 (d) 29 (b) 30 (d) 31 (c) 32 (c) 33 (d) 34 (b)35 (c) 36 (b)

37. Out of the following poisons which works as an anti-coagulant for the control of rats?
    (a) Zinc phosphide (b) Strychmine
    (c) Warfarin (d) Parathion

38. Piercing and sucking type of mouth parts are found in
   (a) Grasshopper (b) House fly
   (c) Aphids (d) Beetles

39. The gland which produces pheromone in queen honey bee
   (a) Mandibular gland (b) Maxillary gland
   (c) Labial gland (d) Pharyngeal gland

40. The legless young of a housefly is known as
   (a) Caterpillar (b) Nymph
   (c) Maggot (d) Grub

41. The paralysis of honey bees is caused by
   (a) Bacteria (c) Fungus
   (b) Virus (d) Mycoplasma

42. The queen in the honey colony feeds on
   (a) Royal jelly (b) Nectar
   (c) Queen substance (d) Honey

43. Which insecticide is stored in the fat of milch animals?
   (a) Malathion (b) Lindane
   (c) DDT (d) Endosulfan

44. Blue green algae are
   (a) Actinomycetes (b) Acellular
   (c) Prokaryotes (d) Eukaryotes

45. Photosynthesis is a
   (a) Catabolic process (b) Anabolic process
   (c) Endergonic process (d) Exergonic process

Answers 37 (c) 38 (c) 39 (a) 40 (c) 41 (b) 42 (a) 43 (c) 44 (c) 45 (a)

46. The real force causing entry of water into a cell from other cell is
   (a) Diffusion pressure deficit (b) Turgor pressure
   (c) Osmotic pressure (d) Wall pressure

47. Which one of the following will reduce the rate of transpiration?
   (a) Increase in windy velocity (b) Rise in temperature
   (c) Increase in water uptake by plants (d) Decrease in light intensity

48. Cell organelle found only in plants is

(a) Mitochondria (b) Golgi complex
(c) Ribosomes (d) Plastids

49. Seeds swell when placed in water due to

(a) Osmosis (b) Respiration
(c) Photosynthesis (d) Imbibition

50. Enzymes are basically

(a) Vitamins (b) Fats
(c) Proteins (d) Carbon

51. A chromosome with median position of centromere is known as

(a) Metacentric (b) Sub metacentric
(c) Telecentric (d) Acrocentric

52. Pseudo-dominance is associated with

(a) Translocations (b) Duplications
(c) Deletions (d) Inversions

53. Haploids which develop from a normal diploid species are referred to as

(a) Monohaploids (b) Polyhaploids
(c) Dihaploids (d) Disomic haploids

54. An individual lacking one chromosome from the diploid set is referred to as

(a) Nullisomic (b) Monosomic
(c) Trisomic (d) Tetrasomic

Answers 46 (a) 47 (d) 48 (d) 49 (d) 50 (c) 51 (a) 52 (c) 53 (a) 54 (b)

55. Laws of inheritance were discovered by Mendel in 1866, while working with

(a) Drosophila (b) Maize
(c) Garden pea (d) Neurospora

56. Crossing over takes place during

(a) Leptotene (b) Zygotene
(c) Pachytene (d) Diplotene

57. Sex chromosomes are also known as

(a) Autosomes (b) Allosomes
(c) Lysosomes (d) Ribosomes

58. In a DNA molecule, thymine always pairs with
   (a) Adenine (b) Guanine
   (c) Cytosine (d) Uracil

59. In RNA molecule, uracil is present in place of
   (a) Adenine (b) Guanine
   (c) Thymine (d) Cytosine

60. Self pollination refers to
   (a) Allogamy (b) Autogamy
   (c) Dichogamy (d) Herkogamy

61. The most effective method for the transfer of oligogenic characters is
   (a) Pedigree breeding (b) Bulk breeding
   (c) Backcross breeding (d) Disruptive mating

62. Hybrid progeny from a cross between two inbreds is known as
   (a) Single cross hybrid (b) Double cross hybrid
   (c) Three way cross hybrid (d) Multiple cross hybrid

63. In India, the crop in which a hybrid variety was the first to be developed is
   (a) Maize (b) Pearlmillet
   (c) Sorghum (d) Cotton

Answers 55 (c) 56 (c) 57 (b) 58 (a) 59 (c) 60 (b) 61 (c) 62 (a) 63 (a)

64. India's rank in rice production in the world is
   (a) First (b) Second
   (c) Third (d) Fourth

65. Causal organism of leaf rust in wheat is
   (a) *Puccinia striformis* (b) *Puccinia graminis pv. Tritici*
   (c) *Puccinia recondita pv. Tritici* (d) *Puccinia maydis*

66. Sunflower originated in
   (a) India (b) China
   (c) Mexico (d) USA Centre of origin

67. Green leaf hopper of paddy is the primary vector of
   (a) Tungro disease (b) Sheath rot
   (c) Kresek disease (d) Ufra disease

68. Erwinia amylovora causes
   (a) Black leg of potato (b) Black arm of cotton
   (c) Fire blight of pear and apple (d) Bacterial blight of bean

69. An organism that is usually parasitic but may also live as saprophyte is called
   (a) Facultative parasite (b) Obligate parasite
   (c) Facultative saprophyte (d) Saprophyte

70. The viruses that are incapable of replicating in their host cells without another virus is called
   (a) Satellite virus (b) Provirus
   (c) Helper virus (d) Virusoids

71. In India, agricultural income is calculated through
   (a) Output method (b) Income method
   (c) Expenditure method (d) Commodity flow method

72. Any parasitic that cannot survive in a dead host and therefore keeps it alive is called
   (a) Necrotroph (b) Hemibiotroph
   (c) Perthotroph (d) Biotroph

Answers 64 (b) 65 (c) 66 (d) 67 (a) 68 (c) 69 (c) 70 (d) 71 (a) 72 (d)

73. Wild fire toxin (tabtoxin) is released/produced by
   (a) *Pseudomonas syringae* (b) *Fusarium oxvsporum*
   (c) *Alternaria alternate* (d) *Pyricularia oryzae*

74. Which organism commonly affects tomato, cotton and banana?
   (a) *Alternaria solani* (b) *Fusarium moniliforme*
   (c) *Furasrium oxysporium* (d) *Erysiphe graminicola*

75. The two important diseases of sugarcane
   (a) Little leaf and bacterial wilt (b) Red rot and grassy shoot
   (c) Red rot and bunt (d) Bakanae disease and stem canker

76. The best soil for tomato growing is
   (a) Sandy soil (b) Loam
   (c) Clay (d) Loamy sand

77. Daily mean temperature favourable for successful production of brinjal is
   (a) 5^0 to 10^0 (b) 10^0C to 15^0
   (c) 13^0C to 21^0C (d) None of the above

78. Pungency in chilli is due to
   (a) Capsaicin (b) Glycoprotein
   (c) Cucurbitacin (d) Tannins

79. Optimum pH of the soil for maximum production of cauliflower is between

(a) 6.0 and 7.0 (b) 4.5 and 5.5

(c) 5.5 and 6.6 (d) None of the above

80. Japanese white is a variety of

(a) Carrot (b) Radish

(c) Turnip (d) None of the above

81. Rat tail or mongri radish belong the botanical variety

(a) Raplanistroides (b) Caudatus

(c) Oleifera (d) Radicula

Answers 73 (a) 74 (c) 75 (b) 76 (b) 77 (c) 78 (a) 79 (c) 80 (b) 81 (b)

82. Number of irrigations required for raising good crop of onion ranges from

(a) 2-4 (b) 5-10

(c) 10-15 (d) 15-20

83. Peas are very rich in

(a) Carbohydrates (b) Protein

(c) Fats (d) Minerals

84. Nitrogen fixation from air through symbiosis is brought about by the bacteria

(a) Rhizobium japonicum (b) Rhizobium leguminosarum

(c) Xanthomonas (d) Mesorhizobium

85. Seed rate per acre for growing cucumber is

(a) 250 g (b) 500 g

(c) 1kg (d) 1.5kg

86. For controlling weeds in okra crop, apply Stomp one day after sowing at the rate of

(a) 500 ml/acre (b) 750 ml/acre

(c) One litre/acre (d) 1.5litre/acre

87. What is the botanical name of garlic?

(a) Allium cepa (b) Allium sativum

(c) Allium capitata (d) Allium garlic

88. Which pest is not harmful to musk melon?

(a) Red pumpkin beetle (b) Epilachna beetle

(c) Fruit fly (d) Red mite

89. Which is not a pest of sweet potato?

(a) Sweet potato weevil (b) Sweet potato sphinx

(c) Hairy caterpillar (d) Aphid

90. Which is the most fertile soil?

(a) Mollisol (b) Ultisol

(c) Alfisol (d) Inceptisol

Answers 82 (c) 83 (b) 84 (b) 85 (c) 86 (c) 87 (b) 88 (d) 89 (c) 90 (a)

91. Brix percentage of sauce is

(a) 16 (b) 20

(c) 25 (d) 32

92. Mango belongs to the family

(a) Leguminaceae (b) Anacardiaceae

(c) Poaceae (d) Compositae

93. Which of the following is the most important pest of mango

(a) Mango hopper (b) Mealy bug

(c) Stem borer (d) Fruit fly

94. Rose species suitable to Northern India climate

(a) *Rosa barbantia* (b) *Rosa multiflora*

(c) *Rosa indica* (d) *Rosa damasina*

95. Blanching is commonly practiced the cultivation of

(a) Chines (b) Cabbage

(c) Broccol (d) Cauliflower

96. The best soil for potato cultivation is

(a) Sandy loam (b) Loamy sand

(c) Clay loam (d) Silty loam

97. Urea contains

(a) 40% Nitrogen (b) 46% Nitrogen

(c) 52% Nitrogen (d) 56% Nitrogen

98. Which of the following is a multi-cut fodder?

(a) Alfalfa (b) Maize

(c) Bajra (d) Cowpea

99. The law of diminishing returns is applicable to

(a) Agriculture (b) Mining
(c) Manufacturing (d) Shipping

100. Which committee recommended introduction of an agricultural tax?

(a) Jha (b) Raj
(c) Chelliah (d) Lakadwala

Answers 91 (d) 92 (b) 93 (a) 94 (c) 95 (d) 96 (a) 97 (b) 98 (c) 99 (a) 100 (b)

State Public Service Commission (Manipur AAO-2015)

1. Which one of the following is a selective herbicide?
   (a) Paraquat (b) Glyphosate
   (c) Atrazine (d) Diquat

2. Zygogramma bicolorata insect is used to control
   (a) *Parthenium hysterophorus* (b) *Echinochloa colonum*
   (c) *Lantana camara* (d) *Orobanche cernua*

3. How is Fluchloralin applied?
   (a) Pre-emergence (b) Post-emergence
   (c) Pre-plant incorporation (d) Late post emergence

4. Which of the following is parasitic weed of lucerne?
   (a) Cuscuta spp. (b) Avena fatua
   (c) Cichorium intybus (d) Cyperus rotundus

5. Mulching is an example of
   (a) Chemical weed control method (b) Biological weed control method
   (c) Mechanical weed control method (d) None of the above

6. Maximum number of seeds per plant are produced by the weed plant
   (a) *Amarnathus* spp. (b) *Argemone mexicana*
   (c) *Cuscuta* spp. (d) *Chenopodium album*

7. Which of the following is contact, non-selective and zero persistent herbicide?
   (a) Fluchloralin (b) 2, 4-D
   (c) Atrazine (d) Paraquat

8. Effective weed control measure of crop associated and crop bound weeds is?
   (a) Intercropping (b) Mulching
   (c) Hoeing & Weeding (d) Crop rotation

9. Example of aquatic weed is?
   (a) *Eichhornia crassipes* (b) *Eleusine indica*
   (c) *Circium arvense* (d) *Amaranthus viridis*

Answers 1 (c) 2 (a) 3 (c) 4 (a) 5 (d) 6 (d) 7 (d) 8 (d) 9 (b)

10. Example of biennial weed is?
    (a) *Cynodon dactyton* (b) *Chenopodium* spp.
    (c) *Cyperus esculentus* (d) *Cirsium vulgare*

11. Field capacity is the ______ limit of soil water availability to plants
    (a) Lower (b) Middle
    (c) Upper (d) All

12. Available Water Holding Capacity is
    (a) Field Capacity-Permanent Wilting Point
    (b) Permanent Wilting Point- Hygroscopic Water
    (c) Field Capacity-Hygroscopic Water
    (d) Field Capacity-Ultimate Wilting Point

13. Which criterion of irrigation scheduling is more suitable and convenient to farmers?
    (a) Soil moisture tension (b) Pan evaporation
    (c) Water potential of plant (d) Critical growth stages

14. Irrigation Requirement (IR) can be obtained by
    (a) IR = Water requirement
    (b) IR = Water requirement + Effective rainfall
    (c) IR = Water requirement – (Effective rainfall + Contribution from ground water table)
    (d) IR = Effective rainfall – (Water requirement + Contribution from ground water table)

15. Limits of boron irrigation waters for semi-tolerant crops varies in between
    (a) 0.3 – 1.0 ppm (b) 1.0 – 3.0 ppm
    (c) 2.0 – 4.0 ppm (d) 4.0 – 6.0 ppm

16. Most important critical growth stage of wheat for irrigation is
    (a) Crown root initiation (b) Tillering
    (c) Jointing (d) Grain filling

17. Water requirement of maize crop is

(a) 100 to 500 mm (b) 500 to 800 mm

(c) 800 to 1500 mm (d) 1500 to 1800 mm

18. Single Super Phosphate contains _________ per cent sulphur

(a) 16 (b) 18

(c) 12 (d) 20

Answers 10 (d) 11 (c) 12 (a) 13 (d) 14 (c) 15 (b) 16 (a) 17 (b) 18 (c)

19. Which one fertilizer contains secondary nutrient other than primary nutrients?

(a) Ammonium nitrate (b) Urea

(c) DAP (d) Ammonium sulphate

20. Which nutrient is essential to increase protein content in cereals?

(a) Phosphorus (b) Nitrogen

(c) Potassium (d) Calcium

21. Which one of the following nutrient stimulates flowering and seed formation?

(a) Nitrogen (b) Phosphorus

(c) Sulphur (d) Calcium

22. Khaira disease in rice is caused by deficiency of

(a) Nitrogen (b) Sulphur

(c) Iron (d) Zinc

23. Which nutrient is not a constituent of chlorophyll but helps in chlorophyll?

(a) Phosphorus (b) Magnesium

(c) Sulphur (d) Nitrogen

24. Which nutrient is essential for symbiotic and non-symbiotic nitrogen fixation?

(a) Boron (b) Zinc

(c) Iron (d) Molybdenum

25. Iron chlorosis in calcareous soils can be corrected by application of

(a) Elemental sulphur (b) Lime

(c) Murate of potash (d) Calcium ammonium nitrate

26. For foliar spray the biuret content in urea should be

(a) 1.0 - 1.5 per cent (b) 1.5 - 2.0 per cent

(c) 2.0 -2.5 per cent (d) Less than 0.5 per cent

27. Whiptail disease of cauliflower is caused by deficiency of

(a) Zinc (b) Molybdenum

(c) Boron (d) Manganese

Answers 19 (d) 20 (b) 21 (b) 22 (d)23 (c) 24 (d) 25 (a) 26 (d) 27 (b)

28. Which one of the following oilcakes contains maximum nitrogen content?
    (a) Castor cake (b) Groundnut cake
    (c) Neem cake (d) Coconut cake

29. Which one of the following is concentrated organic manure?
    (a) FYM (b) Super Compost
    (c) Rock Compost (d) Castor cake

30. Phosphorus fixation is more in
    (a) Neutral soils (b) Acid soils
    (c) Submerged soils (d) None of the above

31. Zinc sulphate should not be mixed with
    (a) SSP (b) Urea
    (c) Ammonium chloride (d) FYM

32. Which one of the following strain of Rhizobium is used in soybean for seed treatment?
    (a) *R. meliloti* (b) *R. trifolii*
    (c) *R. japonicum* (d) *R. leguminoserum*

33. Neem cake contains
    (a) Dhurin (b) Azadirachtin
    (c) Saponin (d) None of these

34. In case of trees and vines the Certificate of Registration shall be valid for
    (a) 6 years (b) 9 years
    (c) 15 years (d) 18 years

35. Desired seed replacement rate for varieties of self and cross pollinated crops are
    (a) 20% and 25% (b) 60% and 50%
    (c) 20% and 10% (d) 25% and 35%

36. A major re-structuring of the seed industry by Government of India through the National Seed Project Phase-III was done in the year
    (a) 1970-71 (b) 1977-78
    (c) 1990-91 (d) 2007-08

Answers 28 (b) 29 (d) 30 (b) 31 (a) 32 (c)33 (b)34 (b) 35 (d) 36 (c)

37. Cytoplasmic-genetic male sterility is controlled by the genes of
    (a) Chloroplast (b) Cytoplasm
    (c) Nucleus (d) Both b and c

38. Loose smut of wheat is
   (a) Externally seed borne (b) Internally seed borne
   (c) Both (a) and (b) (d) None of the above

39. High inbreeding depression is observed in
   (a) Self pollinated crops (b) Often cross pollinated crops
   (c) Cross pollinated crops (d) Not depend on nature of pollination

40. As a result of one meiosis, number of female gametes are formed
   (a) 1 (b) 2
   (c) 3 (d) 4

41. The heterosis can be fixed by
   (a) Apomixes (b) Male sterility
   (c) Self incompatibility (d) None of these

42. Seed is a mature
   (a) Ovary (b) Embryosec
   (c) Ovule (d) Embryo

43. With 'n' heterozygous gene pairs, the proportion of completely homozygous plants after 'm' generations of self-fertilization
   (a) $[(3^m -1)/2^m]^n$ (b) $[(2^m -1)/3^m]^n$
   (c) $[(2^m -1)/2^m]^n$ (d) None of these

44. After 'm' generations of self-fertilization of a complete heterozygous genotype the proportion of homozygosity is
   (a) $(1/2)^m$ (b) $1-(1/2)^m$
   (c) $(1/2)^m - 1$ (d) $1-(1/4)^m$

45. Seed multiplication ratio in Paddy is
   (a) 1 : 100 (b) 1 : 40
   (c) 1 : 80 (d) 1 : 10

Answers 37 (d) 38 (b) 39 (c) 40 (b) 41 (a) 42 (c) 43 (c) 44 (a) 45 (c)

46. Seedlessness in grapes is due to
   (a) Parthenocarpy (b) Embryo abortion
   (c) Polyploidy (d) Lack of pollination

47. For GCA testing the tester should be
   (a) Narrow genetic base (b) Broad genetic base
   (c) Inbred line (d) With dominant genes

48. In back crossing the line to be improved should be used as
 (a) Male recurrent parent (b) Male donor parent
 (c) Female recurrent parent (d) Female donor parent

49. Which one of the following are nonsense codons?
 (a) UUA, AUG, UUU (b) UAC, UUG, UGC
 (c) UAA, UAG, UGA (d) UTA, UTG, UGT

50. Pure line selection is applicable in
 (a) Hybrids (b) Composites
 (c) Synthetics (d) Varieties

51. For seed germination which activity is essential?
 (a) Imbibition of water (b) Cell elongation
 (c) Increase in cell number (d) All of the above

52. The seeds able to tolerate moisture loss
 (a) Recalcitrant (b) Orthodox
 (c) Both a and b (d) None of these

53. Inbred line can be improved by
 (a) Pedigree method (b) Convergent improvement method
 (c) Back crossing (d) All of the above

54. The term gene was coined by
 (a) Mendel (b) Shull
 (c) Bateson (d) Johannsen

Answers 46 (b) 47 (b) 48 (c) 49 (c) 50 (d) 51 (d) 52 (b) 53 (d) 54 (d)

55. In transversion
 (a) Purine replaced by another purine
 (b) Pyrimidine replaced by another pyrimidine
 (c) Purine replaced by pyrimidine or vice versa
 (d) None of these

56. Who described the mutagenic effects of X-rays in barley?
 (a) Muller (1927) (b) Stadler (1928)
 (c) McClintock (1929) (d) None of these

57. Superiority of F_1 over better parent is known as
 (a) Heterosis (b) Heterobeltiosis
 (c) Economic heterosis (d) Luxuriance

58. Segregation occurs during.........

(a) Mitosis (b) Endomitosis

(c) Meiosis (d) All of these

59. In a genome, each type of chromosome is represented.........

(a) Only once (b) Twice

(c) Thrice (d) Many times

60. The chromosomes are most condensed at

(a) Prophase (b) Anaphase

(c) Metaphase (d) Telophase

61. Which of the following seeds can germinate in anaerobic condition?

(a) Wheat (b) Maize

(c) Paddy (d) Green gram

62. The term gene was coined by

(a) Mendel (b) Shull

(c) Bateson (d) Johannsen

63. The tag colour of the foundation seed is

(a) Golden yellow (b) Blue

(c) White (d) Not required

Answers 55 (c) 56 (b) 57 (b) 58 (d) 59 (a) 60 (c) 61 (c) 62 (d) 63 (c)

64. Plants grown in the field from previous crops

(a) Volunteer plants (b) Off-type

(c) Weeds (d) All of the above

65. In maize isolation distance for inbred line from same seed colour plants is

(a) 200 m (b) 400 m

(c) 600 m (d) 800 m

66. Which of the following is cool season crop?

(a) Potato (b) Cucumber

(c) Bean (d) Pumpkin

67. The moisture content for seed storage in wheat should not be more than

(a) 9% (b) 10%

(c) 11% (d) 12%

68. The genetic purity of a variety is tested by

(a) Progeny testing (b) DUS Testing

(c) Grow out test (d) All of the above

69. Based on physiography and climate, the Planning Commission (1985-90) divided the country into _______broad agroclimatic zones

(a) 15 (b) 21

(c) 6 (d) 9

70. The summation of weather conditions over a given region during a comparatively longer period is termed as

(a) Weather (b) Climate

(c) Meteorology (d) None of above

71. The lowermost layer of atmosphere is

(a) Troposhere (b) Stratosphere

(c) Mesosphere (d) Thermosphere

72. For wheat optimal range of temperature for proper germination and vegetative growth is

(a) 21 to 25^0 C (b) 15 to 20^0 C

(c) 10 to 14^0 C (d) 26 to 30^0 C

Answers 64 (d) 65 (b) 66 (a) 67 (d) 68 (d) 69 (a) 70 (b) 71 (a) 72 (a)

73. According to Land Capability Classification, use of Class VI land is restricted to

(a) Field crops (b) Orchards

(c) Field crops and orchards (d) Pastures and siviculture

74. Water in soil above field capacity is termed as

(a) Gravitational water (b) Capillary water

(c) Hygroscopic water (d) None of the above

75. According to USDA system, particle diameter of silt is

(a) 0.002 to 0.020 mm (b) 0.02 to 0.20 mm

(c) 0.20 to 2.00 mm (d) > 2.00 mm

76. In most mineral soils the particle density varies between

(a) 1.4 – 1.8 mg/m^3 (b) 2.5 – 2.7 mg/m^3

(c) 2.0 – 2.2 mg/m^3 (d) 1.8- 2.0 mg/m^3

77. How much area in the country is affected by wind erosion?

(a) 57.16 million ha (b) 2.68 million ha

(c) 10.46 million ha (d) 6.32 million ha

78. The major portion of the soil carried by the wind moves in a series of short bounces is called

(a) Saltation (b) Suspension
(c) Surface creep (d) None of the above

79. Which is a correct sequence of soil erosion?

(a) Sheet-Rill-Gully (b) Rill-Gully-Sheet
(c) Gully-Sheet-Rill (d) Rill-Sheet-Gully

80. If the velocity of water is doubled, its erosive power increases ____times

(a) 2 (b) 4
(c) 6 (d) 8

81. Saltation occurs when particle size is

(a) 0.1-0.5 mm (b) 0.5-1.0 mm
(c) 1.5-2.0 mm (d) 1.0-1.5 mm

Answers 73 (d) 74 (a) 75 (a) 76 (b) 77 (c) 78 (a) 79 (a) 80 (b) 81 (a)

82. Infiltration of soils having hard pan can be increased by

(a) Mulching (b) Sub soiling
(c) Basin listing (d) None of the above

83. The centre of origin of rice is

(a) India and Burma (b) America
(c) South Africa (d) Brazil

84. Boro crop of rice is sown in the month of

(a) May-June (b) June-July
(c) November-December (d) March-April

85. PRH-10 is a hybrid of

(a) Pearlmillet (b) Maize
(c) Sorghum (d) Rice

86. In nursery raised by "Dapog Method" seedlings becomes ready for transplanting at the age of?

(a) 14 days (b) 21 days
(c) 25 days (d) 30 days

87. Six rowed barley is

(a) *Hordeum distichon* (b) *Hordeum vulgare*
(c) *Hordeum irregular* (d) *All of the above*

88. Sweet corn is

(a) *Zea mays indentata* (b) *Zea mays indurata*

(c) *Zea mays saccharata* (d) *Zea mays amylacea*

89. Maize protein 'Zein' is deficient in

(a) Tryptophan and Lysine (b) Vitamin A

(c) Riboflavin (d) Vitamin E

90. Sorghum is considered as camel crop because of

(a) Deep root system (b) Resistance to drought

(c) Shallow root system (d) Nutrient exhaustiveness

Answers 82 (b) 83 (a) 84 (c) 85 (d) 86 (a) 87 (b) 88 (c) 89 (a) 90 (b)

91. Phalaris minor in wheat can be controlled by herbicide

(a) 2, 4-D (b) Atrazine

(c) Paraquat (d) Isoproturon

92. Norin-10 gene is responsible for dwarfism in

(a) Wheat (b) Rice

(c) Black gram (d) Pearl millet

93. Which of the following is ideal temperature for tillering in wheat?

(a) 10-15^{0}C (b) 16-20^{0}C

(c) 20-23^{0}C (d) 23-25^{0}C

94. The recommended seed rate for bunch type groundnut is

(a) 40-50 kg/ha (b) 50-60 kg/ha

(c) 60-70 kg/ha (d) 80-100 kg/ha

95. Which herbicide can be used to control weeds in soybean at 15-20 days after sowing?

(a) Alachlor (b) Imazethapyr

(c) Fluchloralin (d) Metolachlor

96. Recommended depth of sowing for soybean is

(a) 2 to 3 cm (b) 3 to 4 cm

(c) 5 to 6 cm (d) 6 to 8 cm

97. The center of origin of sesame is

(a) America (b) India

(c) South Africa (d) Indonesia

98. The fruit of mustard is
   (a) Siliqua (b) Receme
   (c) Caryopsis (d) Ear

99. Delinting of cotton seed can be done with
   (a) Hydrochloric acid (b) Nitric acid
   (c) Sulphuric acid (d) Citric acid

Answers 91 (d) 92 (a) 93 (b) 94 (d) 95 (b) 96 (b) 97 (b) 98 (a) 99 (c)

100. In sugarcane setts hot water treatment is done to
   (a) Control seed borne diseases (b) Control soil borne diseases
   (c) Break dormancy (d) Convert sucrose into glucose

101. Cuscuta is a parasitic weed of
   (a) Berseem (b) Lucerne
   (c) Oat (d) Fodder sorghum

102. The metamorphic rock, marble is formed from
   (a) Limestone (b) Sandstone
   (c) Shale (d) Coal

103. Which crop grows in high pH soil?
   (a) Banana (b) Amla
   (c) Papaya (d) Mandarin

104. Science which deals with soils genesis and classification
   (a) Petrology (b) Pedagogy
   (c) Pedology (d) Petrography

105. Which is the soil order of deep black soil?
   (a) Vertisols (b) Entisols
   (c) Inceptisols (d) Ultisols

106. Arrangements of soil particles is referred as
   (a) Soil texture (b) Soil structure
   (c) Soil organization (d) None of the above

107. First 15 cm layer of land which is ploughed for cultivation of crop is called
   (a) Soil profile (b) Rhizosphere soil
   (c) Furrow slice (d) Sub-soil

108. Soil particles get deflocculated due to presence of
   (a) Sulphur (b) Sodium
   (c) Calcium (d) Magnesium

Answers 100 (a) 101(b) 102 (a) 103 (b) 104 (c) 105 (a) 106 (b) 107(c) 108 (b)

109. Which of the following crop has been approved for commercial cultivation in India?
   (a) Bt. Brinjal (b) Bt. Tomato
   (c) Bt. Cotton (d) None of the above

110. Which of the following does not apply to SRI method of rice cultivation?
   (a) Reduced water application (b) Reduced plant density
   (c) Reduced age of seedlings (d) Increased application of fertilizers

111. Cotton belongs to the family
   (a) Cruciferae (b) Malvaceae
   (c) Anacardiaceae (d) Solanaceae

112. A bud mutant cultivar of mango is
   (a) Noorjahan (b) Rosica
   (c) Creton (d) Ratna

113. "Arka Mridula" is a variety of
   (a) Tamarind (b) Mango
   (c) Guava (d) Apple

114. Parentage of "Amrapali" hybrid of mango are
   (a) Neelum x Dashehari (b) Dashehari x Neelum
   (c) Neelum x Alphonso (d) Ratna x Alphonso

115. Grape is mostly propagated by
   (a) Inarching (b) Budding
   (c) Soft wood grafting (d) Hard wood stem cutting

116. _____ is propagated by off-shoots (suckers) emerging from the base of the plant?
   (a) Mandarin (b) Guava
   (c) Date Palm (d) Pomegranate

117. Ideal planting distance of Date palm is
   (a) 5m × 5m (b) 6m × 6m
   (c) 7m × 7m (d) 8m × 8m

Answers 109 (c) 110 (d) 111 (b) 112 (b) 113 (c) 114 (b) 115 (d) 116 (c) 117 (d)

118. "Pusa Delicious" is a variety of
(a) Date Palm (b) Papaya
(c) Banana (d) Mango

119. In Central India, mandarins are manured during May for
(a) Mrig Bahar (b) Ambe Bahar
(c) Hast Bahar (d) None of the above

120. January–February flowering in Pomegranate is known as
(a) Mrig Bahar (b) Ambe Bahar
(c) Hasta Bahar (d) None of these

121. "NA 6" variety of Aonla is a selection of
(a) Chakaiya (b) Francis
(c) Banarasi (d) NA 7

122. 'Seb' is a popular variety of
(a) Coconut (b) Date palm
(c) Ber (d) Cashew nut

123. In high density orcharding of papaya with variety Pusa Nanha, suitable plant spacing is
(a) 1.2 m × 1.2 m (b) 1.6 m × 1.6 m
(c) 1.8 m × 1.8 m (d) 1.0 m × 1.0 m

124. Panama wilt disease in Banana is caused by
(a) *M. phaseolina* (b) *Fusarium oxysporum*
(c) *G. musae* (d) *V. theobromae*

125. Powdery mildew in Ber is caused by
(a) *I. zizyphi* (b) *Alternaria spp.*
(c) *Phytophthora* spp. (d) *Oidium zizyphi*

126. Causal organism for Gummosis in Citrus is
(a) *Phytophthora* spp. (b) *Xanthomonas* spp.
(c) *Alternaria citri* (d) *Glomerella cingulata*

Answers 118 (b) 119 (a) 120 (b) 121 (a) 122 (c) 123 (a) 124 (b) 125 (d) 126 (a)

127. Ideal time for T-budding in roses in northern plains is
(a) February – April (b) January – March
(c) December – February (d) October – November

128. 'Pusa Uttam' is a variety of

(a) Tomato (b) Potato
(c) Bottle gourd (d) Brinjal

129. Average seed rate of cabbage is

(a) 500 -750 g (b) 200-350 g
(c) 1000-1250 g (d) 350-450 g

130. Which one is a rich source of carotene?

(a) Brinjal (b) Cauliflower
(c) Carrot (d) Capsicum

131. Scientific name of cauliflower is

(a) *Brassica oleracea var. botrytis* (b) *Brassica oleracea var. capitata*
(c) *Brassica oleracea var. gemmifera* (d) *Brassica oleracea var. italica*

132. Crop geometry of spring–summer season okra is

(a) 60 cm × 30 cm (b) 45cm × 30 cm
(c) 60 cm × 60 cm (d) 60 cm × 45 cm

133. Pusa Chetki is a variety of

(a) Radish (b) Carrot
(c) Cauliflower (d) Cabbage

134. How much area is required for raising seedlings of tomato for one hectare?

(a) 1000 m^2 (b) 750 m^2
(c) 500 m^2 (d) 250 m^2

135. Optimum seed rate of small seeded water melon is

(a) 3.0 – 3.5 kg/ha (b) 2.0 – 2.5 kg/ha
(c) 4.0 – 4.5 kg/ha (d) 1.0 –1.5 kg/ha

Answers 127(c) 128 (d) 129 (d) 130 (c) 131 (a) 132 (b) 133 (a) 134 (d) 135 (a)

136. Damping off in chilli is caused by

(a) *Pythium* spp. (b) *Erysiphe* spp.
(c) *Peronospora* spp. (d) *Albugo* spp.

137. Causal organism of powdery mildew in pea

(a) *Septoria lycopersici* (b) *Uromyces pisi*
(c) *Erysiphe polygoni* (d) *Fusarium* spp.

138. Radical cracks at the stem end of the tomato fruit are caused by

(a) Phosphorus deficiency (b) Phytophthora infestans
(c) Fruit borer (d) Wide fluctuations in soil moisture

139. In cabbage, cauliflower and broccoli hollow stems with darkened interiors are most often caused by

(a) Boron deficiency (b) Magnesium deficiency
(c) Calcium deficiency (d) Chilling temperature

140. Thread like white lines on the vegetable leaf that gradually widen are symptom of

(a) Aphids (b) Flea beetles
(c) Army worm feeding (d) Leaf miner

141. Soft wood grafting is successful in

(a) Grapes (b) Aonla
(c) Pomegranate (d) Mango

142. Fruit drop is controlled by:

(a) IBA (b) NAA
(c) IAA (d) GA_3

143. Which of the following is not an auxin?

(a) IAA (b) NAA
(c) 2, 4-D (d) GA_3

144. If heritability is high which method is most suitable?

(a) Mass selection (b) Half sib selection
(c) Full sib selection (d) Reciprocal recurrent selection

Answers 136(c) 137 (c) 138 (d) 139 (a) 140 (d) 141 (b) 142 (b) 143 (d) 144 (d)

145. The natural selection can play the role in

(a) Pure line selection (b) Pedigree selection
(c) Bulk method (d) Single seed descent method

146. Proportion of individuals having the expected phenotype determined by particular gene is called

(a) Expressivity (b) Heritability
(c) Segregation (d) Penetrance

147. A, B, AB and O blood groups are the example of

(a) Pleiotropy (b) Heritability
(c) Dominance (d) Codominance

148. Homozygous population includes.........

(a) Pure lines (b) Inbred lines
(c) Multi lines (d) All of these

149. The classical gene-for-gene hypothesis was proposed by
    (a) Flor, 1956 (b) Painte, 1951
    (c) Robinson, 1969 (d) Hayes, 1947

150. 9:3:4 Ratio is obtained in
    (a) Recessive epistasis (b) Dominant epistasis
    (c) Duplicate epistasis (d) Complementary epistasis

Answers 145 (c) 146 (d) 147 (d) 148 (d) 149 (a) 150 (a)

Selective Questions (FAQ)

1. The first Sugar Mill in India was set up in 1903 at
   (a) Partapgarh (b) Pratappur
   (c) Mawana (d) Balrampur
2. India's rank in rice production in the world is
   (a) First (b) Second
   (c) Third (d) Fourth
3. First interspecific hybrid was developed by Thomas Fairchild (1717) between
   (a) *Tagetus erecta* and *Tegetus patula*
   (b) *Dianthus Caryophyllus* and *Dianthus barbatus*
   (c) *Chrysanthemum carinatum* and *Chrysanthemum coronarium*
   (d) *Chrysanthemum segetum* and *Chrysanthemum carinatum*
4. How much area is required for raising nursery for planting one hectare of rice?
   (a) 1/5 of total area (b) 1/10 of total area
   (c) 1/15 of total area (d) 1/20 of total area
5. Rice Gandhibug is scientifically known as
   (a) *Oresalia oryzea* (b) *Leptocorisa acutea*
   (c) *Benesia taba* (d) None
6. The rice varieties grown in India belong to
   (a) Indica (b) Japonica
   (c) Javanica (d) Asiatica
7. The rice inflorescence is known as
   (a) Panicle (b) Spikelet
   (c) Ear (d) Siliqua

8. For transplanting one hectare area of rice how much area is sufficient for nursery raising?

(a) $100m^2$ (b) $500m^2$

(c) $1000m^2$ (d) $1500m^2$

9. Tungro virus of rice is transmitted by

(a) Stem borer (b) Green leaf hopper

(c) Leaf roller (d) White fly

Answers 1 (b) 2 (b) 3 (b) 4 (b) 5 (b) 6 (a) 7 (a) 8 (c) 9 (b)

10. In which of the following crops azolla is used as bio-fertilizer?

(a) Rice (b) Sorghum

(c) Sunflower (d) Maize

11. Khaira disease in rice is caused due to

(a) Fungal infection (b) Bacterial infection

(c) Zinc deficiency (d) Boron deficiency

12. The State of India having highest area under rice crop is

(a) Bihar (b) Punjab

(c) Kerala (d) West Bengal

13. The sowing time of the Boro rice grown in West Bengal is

(a) May-June (b) June-July

(c) January-February (d) September-October

14. Which of the following variety of rice is a cross between IR262 and TKM6 evolved at IRRI, Philippines?

(a) IR 8 (b) Pusa 2-21

(c) IR 20 (d) Ratna

15. Jaya and Ratna rice varieties contain the dwarfing genes from

(a) Dee-geo-woo-gen (b) Norin 8

(c) Spontaneous mutation (d) Induced mutation

16. IR 8 varieties of Rice was developed at

(a) CRRI Cuttack (b) IRRI, Philippines

(c) Taiwan (d) Japan

17. Rice flower has how many stamens?

(a) 6 (b) 4

(c) 3 (d) 8

18. The stable food crop of Southern India is
(a) Wheat (b) Bajra
(c) Jowar (d) Rice

Answers 10 (a) 11 (c) 12 (d) 13 (c)14 (c) 15 (a) 16 (b) 17 (a) 18 (d)

19. Rice belongs to the family
(a) Leguminaceae (b) Poaceae
(c) Malvaceae (d) Solanaceae

20. Father of Hybrid Rice
(a) Prof. Yuvan Long Ping (b) Dr. N. E. Borlaugh
(c) Dr. M. S. Swaminathan (d) Dr. G. S. Kush

21. Golden rice is enriched with
(a) Vitamin B1 (b) Vitamin D
(c) Vitamin C (d) Vitamin A

22. The safe grain moisture content for storage of rice
(a) 14% (b) 16%
(c) 18% (d) 20%

23. Which of the crop is self pollinated?
(a) Millets (b) Onion
(c) Rice (d) Cotton

24. Brown Plant Hopper is a pest of
(a) Sorghum (b) Wheat
(c) Rice (d) Maize

25. Rice prefers Nitrogen in the form of
(a) Nitrate (b) Amide
(c) Ammoniacal (d) Nitrous

26. Decomposition of organic matter in rice soils generate
(a) Ethane (b) Methane
(c) Propane (d) Butane

27. The area required for DAPOG nursery for sowing 1 hectare rice is
(a) 50 m^2 (b) 30 m^2
(c) 100 m^2 (d) 10 m^2

Answers 19 (b) 20 (a) 21 (d) 22 (a) 23 (c)24 (c)25 (c) 26 (b) 27 (c)

28. The seed rate (kg/ha) of hybrid rice is
    (a) 25 kg/ha (b) 5 k/ha
    (c) 45 kg/h (d) 15 kg/ha

29. India's rank in rice production in the world is
    (a) First (b) Second
    (c) Third (d) Fourth

30. The centre of origin of rice is
    (a) India and Burma (b) America
    (c) South Africa (d) Brazil

31. Boro crop of rice is sown in the month of
    (a) May-June (b) June-July
    (c) November-December (d) March-April

32. PRH-10 is a hybrid of
    (a) Pearlmillet (b) Maize
    (c) Sorghum (d) Rice

33. In nursery raised by "Dapog Method" seedlings becomes ready for transplanting at the age of?
    (a) 14 days (b) 21 days
    (c) 25 days (d) 30 days

34. Which of the following does not apply to SRI method of rice cultivation?
    (a) Reduced water application (b) Reduced plant density
    (c) Reduced age of seedlings (d) Increased application of fertilizers

35. The fruit of wheat is known as
    (a) Pod (b) Capsule
    (c) Siliqua (d) Caryopsis

36. Triticale and interspecific hybrid between Wheat and Rye was developed by
    (a) Knight (1800) (b) Rimpu (1890)
    (c) Davenport (1908) (d) Sewall Wright (1921)

Answers 28 (d) 29 (b) 30 (a) 31 (c) 32 (d) 33 (a) 34 (d) 35 (d) 36 (b)

37. Dwarf wheat (Mexican) is introduced in India by
    (a) Dr. N.E. Borlaug (b) Dr. M.S. Swaminathan
    (c) Dr. B.P. Pal (d) Dr. C. Subramaniam

38. The normal seed rate of wheat is
 (a) 50 kg/ha (b) 75 kg/ha
 (c) 100 kg/ha (d) 125 kg/ha

39. Triticale is a cross between
 (a) Wheat × oat (b) Wheat × barley
 (c) Oat × barley (d) Wheat × Rye

40. Which of the following crop rotation is the best for maintaining soil fertility?
 (a) Maize-toria-wheat (b) Paddy-wheat-maize
 (c) Paddy-potato-greengram (d) Soyabean-wheat-greengram

41. Loose smut of wheat is
 (a) Externally seed borne (b) Internally seed borne
 (c) Both (a) and (b) (d) None of the above

42. The maximum production of wheat is in
 (a) Maharashtra (b) Punjab
 (c) M.P. (d) U.P.

43. Recommended depth of sowing for dwarf wheat varieties is
 (a) 5 cm (b) 9 cm
 (c) 3 cm (d) 7.5 cm

44. Which one of the following is a variety of wheat crop?
 (a) PR-116 (b) PBW550
 (c) PMH-1 (d) SML668

45. Which of the following restricts coverage of wheat in India?
 (a) Photoperiod (b) Temperature
 (c) Light intensity (d) Irrigation

Answers 37 (a) 38 (c) 39 (d) 40 (d) 41 (b) 42 (d) 43 (a) 44 (b) 45 (d)

46. PBW 343 is a popular variety of.........
 (a) Rice (b) Maize
 (c) Barley (d) Wheat

47. The Mexican wheat varieties introduced in India in 1963 were:
 (a) Kayan Sona and Sonalika (b) S 308 and K 68
 (c) Lerma Rojo and Sonera 64 (d) HD 1982 and HD 2122

48. Solar energy treatment of wheat seed is recommended for the control of:
 (a) Loose smut (b) Hill bunt
 (c) Black rust (d) Karnal bunt

49. Leaf rust resistance in wheat (T-aestivum) has been transferred from:
(a) *Triticum monococcum* (b) *Triticum speltoides*
(c) *Triticum timopheevii* (d) All of the above

50. The normal seed rate of wheat is
(a) 50 kg/ha (b) 75 kg/ha
(c) 100 kg/ha (d) 125 kg/ha

51. Kalyan sona is a variety of
(a) Wheat (b) Rye
(c) Barley (d) Oat

52. Major type of wheat cultivated in India
(a) *Triticum diurum* (b) *Triticum aestivum*
(c) *Triticum sphaerococum* (d) *All the above*

53. Most commonly used herbicide to kill broad leaf weeds in wheat field is
(a) Alachlor (b) Atrazin
(c) 2-4-D (d) Isoproturon

54. Loose smut of wheat is a disease
(a) Internally seed borne (b) Air borne
(c) Soil borne (d) Externally seed borne

Answers 46 (d) 47 (a) 48 (a) 49 (d) 50 (c) 51 (a) 52 (b) 53 (c) 54 (a)

55. Phalaris minor is a weed found with
(a) Wheat (b) Cowpea
(c) Barley (d) Oat

56. Causal organism of leaf rust in wheat is
(a) *Puccinia striformis* (b) *Puccinia graminis pv. Tritici*
(c) *Puccinia recondita pv. Tritici* (d) *Puccinia maydis*

57. Most important critical growth stage of wheat for irrigation is
(a) Crown root initiation (b) Tillering
(c) Jointing (d) Grain filling

58. Loose smut of wheat is
(a) Externally seed borne (b) Internally seed borne
(c) Both (a) and (b) (d) None of the above

59. The moisture content for seed storage in wheat should not be more than
(a) 9% (b) 10%
(c) 11% (d) 12%

60. For wheat optimal range of temperature for proper germination and vegetative growth is

(a) 21 to 25°C (b) 15 to 20°C

(c) 10 to 14°C (d) 26 to 30°C

61. Phalaris minor in wheat can be controlled by herbicide

(a) 2, 4-D (b) Atrazine

(c) Paraquat (d) Isoproturon

62. Norin-10 gene is responsible for dwarfism in

(a) Wheat (b) Rice

(c) Black gram (d) Pearl millet

63. Which of the following is ideal temperature for tillering in wheat?

(a) 10-15°C (b) 16-20°C

(c) 20-23°C (d) 23-25°C

Answers 55 (a) 56 (c) 57 (a) 58 (b) 59 (d) 60 (a) 61 (d) 62 (a) 63 (b)

Selective Questions of Horticulture

Q. 1. Parbhani Kranti is a variety of

Ans. Okra

Q. 2. Pusa Kranti is a variety of

Ans. Brinjal

Q. 3. Pusa Barsati, Pusa-do-fasli, Pusa Rituraj are varieties of

Ans. Cowpea

Q. 4. Pusa Meghali is a improved variety of

Ans. Carrot

Q. 5. Varsha Uphar is a variety of

Ans. Okra

Q. 6. Arka Sheel and Pusa Purple Long are varieties of

Ans. Brinjal

Q. 7. Pusa Purple round variety of brinjal is resistant to

Ans. Little leaf of brinjal

Q. 8. Pusa Sawani, Parbhani Kranti nas Pusa Makhamali are varieties of

Ans. Okra

Q. 9. Punjab Padmani and Versha Uphar are varieties of

Ans. Okra

Q. 10. Pusa Rituraj, Pusa Phalguni, Pusa Barsati are varieties of

Ans. Cowpea

Q. 11. Angurlata, Pusa Early Dwarf and Pusa Ruby are varieties of

Ans. Tomato

Q. 12. Pusa Sheetal, Sawrab and Ashish are varieties of

Ans. Tomato

Q. 13. Blue Lake, Arka Komal and Pant Anupama are varieties of

Ans. French bean

Q. 14. Kashmir beauty and Golden heart are varieties of

Ans. Carrot

Q. 15. Pusa Meghali and Early Nantes are varieties of

Ans. Carrot

Q. 16. Pusa Yamdagni is a varieties of

Ans. Carrot

Q. 17. Arka Nishant and Bombay red are varieties of

Ans. Radish

Q. 18. Pusa Meghdoot and Pusa Manjari are varieties of

Ans. Bootle gourd

Q. 19. Durgapura Meetha and Durgapur Kesar are varieties of

Ans. Water melon

Q. 20. Pusa Bendana and Arka Jyoti are varieties of

Ans. Water melon

Q. 21. Jobner Green is a high yielding variety of

Ans. Indian spinach (beet leaf)

Q. 22. Rose Supreme, Happy End and Friendship are varieties of

Ans. Gladiolus

Q. 23. Gladiolus is generally propagated by

Ans. Corm

Q. 24. Oleoresin is extracted from

Ans. Chillies

Q. 25. Japenese Long Green is a popular variety of

Ans. Cucumber

Q. 26. Mangala is an improved variety of

Ans. Arecanut

Q. 27. Vector for Yellow Vein Mosaic of Okra is

Ans. White fly (*Bemisia tabaci*)

Q. 28. Leaf curl virus is generally caused by

Ans. White fly

Q. 29. Rayan is used as root stock for propogation of

Ans. Sapota (Chekoo)

Q. 30. Manikara hexandra is used as rootstock for

Ans. Sapota

Q. 31. *Mangifera indica* is an

Ans. Amphidiploid

Q. 32. Iron deficiency causes

Ans. Lime Induced Chlorosis

Q. 33. Monoembyonic citrus species is

Ans. *Citrus grandis* (Pummelo)

Q. 34. Pusa Majesty and Pusa delicious are monoembryonic varieties of

Ans. Papaya

Q. 35. *Helopeltis antonii* is a serious pest of

Ans. Cashew

Q. 36. Best planting material of Pineapple is

Ans. Slip

Q. 37. Kinnow is a Hybrid between

Ans. *Citrus nobilis* × *Citrus deliciosa*

Q. 38. High density planting in Pinneapple accommodates plants of about

Ans. 60,000/Hac

Q. 39. Bronzing in Guava is due to deficiency of

Ans. Zn

Q. 40. Aroma of overripe fruit of banana is due to

Ans. Isopentanol

Q. 41. Alternative bearing in Mango is controlled by

Ans. Paclobutrazol

Q. 42. Red colour of Plum fruit is due to pigment

Ans. Anthocyanin

Q. 43. Amount of pectin in jelly is tested by

Ans. Jelmeter

Q. 44. Couference and Bartlette are varieties of

Ans. Pear

Q. 45. Bartted max is a variety of

Ans. Apple

Q. 46. Ber (*Ziziphus mauritiana)* belongs to family

Ans. Rhamnaceae

Q. 47. Bael belong to family

Ans. Rutaceae

Q. 48. The rootstock which has most dwarfing effect for grape fruit and oranges are

Ans. *Severinia buxifolia*

Q. 49. Removal of male bud in banana is called

Ans. Denovelling

Q. 50. Cashew Apple juice is rich in Vitamin

Ans. Ascorbic Acid

Q. 51. Vegetative method for the propagation of litchi is

Ans. Marcotting

Q. 52. Root stoch for the propagation of Sapota is

Ans. Rayan

Q. 53. Wine made from Pears is known as

Ans. Perry

Q. 54. Amrich is a variety of

Ans. Apple

Q. 55. Arakta and Bassein Seedless are varieties of

Ans. Pomegranate

Q. 56. Gynodioecious varieties of Papaya are

Ans. Pusa delicious and Pusa Majesty

Q. 57. Training system of apple in India is

Ans. Modified leader

Q. 58. Training system in Peach (Aadoo) is

Ans. Open centre

Q. 59. Fruit cracking in litchi can be controlled by spraying

Ans. 0.4% Borax

Q. 60. Training systems used in grapes are

Ans. Bower and Kniffin

Q. 61. Banana is propagated by

Ans. Sword Suckers

Q. 62. Date palm is propagated by

Ans. Off shoots

Q. 63. Banana variety used for chips making is

Ans. Nandran

Q. 64. Predominant acid in grape is

Ans. Tartaric acid

Q. 65. Kagzhi lime is a better indicator plant than Sweet orange for

Ans. Citrus tristeza virus (CTV)

Q. 66. Zinc deficiency in grapes causes

Ans. Straggly cluster

Q. 67. Internal cork of apple is due to deficiency of

Ans. Boron

Q. 68. Black pod is a disease of

Ans. Cocoa

Q. 69. Rust ring is a disease of

Ans. Aonla

Q. 70. Mutant of Red banana is

Ans. Misri

Q. 71. Beauty seedless variety of grape is a cross of

Ans. Queen of Vineyard × Black Kishmish

Q. 72. Bassein seedless, Arakta and Ganesh are varieties of

Ans. Pomegranate

Q. 73. Cutting of banana pseudo-stem after harvesting is

Ans. Mettocking

Q. 74. Bud dormancy in grape can be broken by

Ans. Hydrogen cynamid

Q. 75. De-greening in citrus is done with the application of

Ans. Ethephon or CEPA (2-Chloro ethyl phosphonic acid)

Q. 76. Calcium carbide releases

Ans. Acetylene

Q. 77. Storage temperature for banana is

Ans. 13^0 C

Q. 78. India's share in world's mango production is

Ans. 57%

Q. 79. Cashew export is rising at the rate of

Ans. 33%

Q. 80. Bael (*Aegle marmelos*) is a rich source of

Ans. Riboflavin (B_2)

Q. 81. *Manilkara Zapota* (Chiko) also known as Sapota is a

Ans. Climacteric fruit

Q. 82. *Ananas comosus* (Pineapple) is a

Ans. Non-climacteric fruit

Q. 83. Ring rust of Aonla is due to

Ans. *Ravenelia emblica*

Q. 84. Sap burn is a post-harvest disorder in

Ans. Mango

Q. 85. Prabhat and Shalimar are varieties of

Ans. Walnut

Q. 86. Amphimixis is a method of

Ans. Sexual reproduction

Q. 87. Pepper is a good intercrop in

Ans. Coconut

Q. 88. 'Ganesh'- a National variety of pomegranate is selected from

Ans. Alandi/Vadke

Q. 89. Rosica is a mutant cultivar of

Ans. Mango

Q. 90. Nematode resistant rootstock of fig is

Ans. *Ficus glomerata*

Q. 91. Domestic quarantine exists in India for

Ans. *Sanjose scale*

Q. 92. Tea mosquito is a serious pest of

Ans. Cashew nut

Q. 93. Wax coating enhances shelf life by blocking

Ans. Transpiration

Q. 94. Clonal selection of mango variety which bears fruits regularly is

Ans. Dashehari-51

Q. 95. Arka Puneet, Arka Aruna, Arka Anmol are varieties of

Ans. Mango

Q. 96. Fruits which shows either a rise in respiration or an associated production of ethylene during ripening process are called

Ans. Climacteric fruits

Q. 97. Climacteric fruits are

Ans. Spota, Plum, Papaya, Banana, Apple, Mango, Avocada, Peach, Plum, Guava, Pear, Tomato, Kiwi, Fig

Q. 98. Fruits which show little or no ethylene production and no large increase in CO_2 production are called

Ans. Non-Climacteric fruits

Q. 99. Non-climacteric fruits are

Ans. Cashew, Pineapple, Lime, Orange, Strawberry, Lychee, Cherry, Malay Apple, Grape

Q. 100. India is the largest producer of

Ans. Ginger, Okra and Chillies

Q. 101. India is the largest producer of

Ans. Mango, Banana, Guava and Papaya

Q. 102. Preservation of tomato ketchup is done by

Ans. Sodium benzoate

Q.103. Central Institute of Sub-tropical Horticulture is located at

Ans. Lucknow

Q. 104. Roopa is an improved variety of

Ans. Walnut

Q. 105. Fruits are blanched before canning at temperature of

Ans. 80°C

Q. 106. Exhausting temperature of canned fruits is

Ans. 80-82°C

Q. 107. Recommended storage temperature to extend shelf life of banana is

Ans. 12-15°C

Q. 108. Country ranked highest in Vegetable production

Ans. India

Q. 109. Mango and Cashew nut belongs to family

Ans. Anacardiaceae

Q. 110. Most important disease of banana in India is

Ans. Bunchy top

Q. 111. Cashew nut and Pineapple originated in

Ans. Brazil

Q. 112. Fruit crop suitable for high soil pH is

Ans. Aonla

Q. 113. Fruit having rich source of fat is

Ans. Walnut

Q. 114. Fruit having rich source of protein is

Ans. Cashew nut

Q. 115. Seedlessness in lemon (Citrus lemon) is due to

Ans. Self-incompatibility

Q. 116. Grape variety which is parthenocarpic

Ans. Black corianth

Q. 117. Requirement of per capta Vegetables/day is

Ans. 300gm

Q. 118. Avalability of per capta Vegetables/day is

Ans. 120gm

Q. 119. Cat-face is a physiological disorder of

Ans. Tomato

Q. 120. Shoot and fruit borer of Okra belong to

Ans. *Earias vitella*

Q. 121. Chemical providing drought resistance in pea

Ans. Chlormequat

Q. 122. Pungency in Carrot is due to volatile compound

Ans. Isothiocyanates

Q. 123. In which vegetable less than 20mg solanine per 100gm fresh weight is considered safe for human consumption

Ans. Potatao

Q. 124. Major pest of potato during storage is

Ans. Potato tuber moth

Q. 125. Pungency in Onion is due to

Ans. Allyl propyl disulphide

Q. 126. Which is the phenolic factor that is present in Onion

Ans. Catechol

Q. 127. Onion bulbs are stored well at a temperature of

Ans. 0°C TO 1°C

Q. 128. Garlic contain the amino acid

Ans. Allin

Q. 129. System used in Onion for hybrid seed production is

Ans. CMS

Q. 130. In India date is harvested at

Ans. Doka stage

Q.131. Which country ranks first in in tomato and potato production?

Ans. China

Q. 132. India's rank in tomato production is

Ans. 2nd

Q. 133. India's rank in potato production is

Ans. 5th

Q. 134. Dehaulming in potato is done by

Ans. $CuSo_4$

Q. 135. In Potato cutting of haulms/aerial parts by sickle or killing by chemicals like Gramoxone when the crop attains 80-90 days and when the aerial part of the plant turns yellow is called

Ans. Dehaulming

Q. 136. Who is the largest producing country of Cabbage and Cauliflower

Ans. China

Q. 137. Type of inflorescence in cabbage is known as

Ans. Catkin

Q. 138. Anticancer properties in cabbage is due to

Ans. Indole-3-cardinal

Q. 139. Tip burn in cabbage is due to

Ans. Ca deficiency

Q. 140. Highest cauliflower producing state is

Ans. West Bengal

Q. 141. Pusa hybrid 2, Pusa Aghani and Snowball are hybrids of

Ans. Cauliflower

Q. 142. pH of soil for maximum production of cauliflower is

Ans. 5.5-6.5

Q. 143. Which country has highest production of Mango?

Ans. India

Q. 144. Which country has highest productivity of Mango in world?

Ans. Venezuela

Q. 145. Good mango varieties have TSS of

Ans. 20%

Q. 146. India's share in banana production in the world is

Ans. 31.7%

Q. 147. Country leading in Apple production is

Ans. China

Q. 148. Kohir safed and Safed jam are hybrid varieties of

Ans. Guava

Q. 149. Papaya is native of

Ans. Tropical America

Q. 150. Largest Papaya producing state in India is

Ans. Andra Pradesh followed by Gujrat

Q. 151. Highest production of Papaya is in

Ans. Brazil

Q. 152. India's rank in Papaya production in the world is

Ans. 4th

Q. 153. Mosambi, Blood Red Malta, Pineapple and Valancia are varieties of

Ans. Sweet orange

Q. 154. Propagating method of Sapota (Chiku) is

Ans. Inarching

Q. 155. Propagating method of Aonla is

Ans. Patch budding

Q. 156. Propagating method of Date palm is

Ans. Off shoot

Q. 157. Requirement of per capita of Fruits/day is

Ans. 120 gm

Q. 158. Availability of per capita of vegetables is

Ans. 70-80 gm

Q. 159. County leading in Litchi and Peaches production is

Ans. China

Q. 160. Country leading in Cherry production is

Ans. Turkey

Q. 161. Leading flower producing country

Ans. Netherlands

Q. 167. Largest flower producing state in India

Ans. Tamil Nadu

Q. 168. Native of Marigold is

Ans. Maxico

Q. 169. Gadiolus belongs to family

Ans. Irridaceae

Q. 170. Thornless variety of Rose is

Ans. Chitra

Q. 171. Inflorecence of Mango and Litchi are called

Ans. Panicle

Selective Questions of Plant Pathology

Q.1. Father of Plant Pthology

Ans. Anton de Bary

Q. 2. Father of modern Plant Pathology in India

Ans. JF Dastur

Q. 3. Father of Insect Physiology

Ans. Wiggleworth

Q. 4. Father of Mycology

Ans. Antoico Michelli

Q. 5. Father of modern Plant Pathology

Ans. Julius Koon

Q. 6. Father of Indian Mycology

Ans. E J Butler

Q. 7. Founder of Virology

Ans. Beijerinck

Q. 8. 1st Indian scientist who collected and identified fungi in India

Ans. K.R. Kirtikar

Q. 9. Loose smut of Wheat and Loose smut of Barley are

Ans. Internally Seed borne diseases

Q. 10. Brown leaf spot of Rice, Red leaf spot of Sugarcane and Ergot of Bajra are

Ans. Internally Seed borne diseases

Q. 11. Downy mildew of Pearl millet and Smut of Pearl millet are

Ans. Soil borne diseases

Q. 12. Early blight of Potato is

Ans. Soil borne disease

Q. 13. Irish famine/Ireland famine of 1845 was due to

Ans. Late blight of Potato (*Phytophthora infestans*)

Q. 14. Bengal famine of 1943 was due to

Ans. Brown leaf spot of Rice (*Helminthosporium oryzae*)

Q. 15. Disease which is prevalent or occurs throughout the country or continent is called

Ans. Pandemic disease

Q. 16. Disease which occur widely but periodically

Ans. Epiphytotic

Q. 17. Disease confined to a particular country or district or location is called

Ans. Endemic

Q. 18. Potato black leg pathogen is caused by

Ans. *Erwinia carotovora*

Q. 19. Bacterial leaf blight can be controlled by

Ans. Streptocycline

Q. 20. Sexual spores of fungi are

Ans. Zygospores

Q. 21. Fungicide which effectively control covered smut of barley is

Ans. Vitavax

Q. 22. Kernel bunt of wheat gives foul smell in the field due to presence of volatile compound

Ans. Trimethyl amine

Q. 23. Bunt or kernel smut of rice is caused by

Ans. *Neovossia horrida*

Q. 24. Spores of *Puccinia graminis tritici* which infect the barberry plant is

Ans. Basidiospores

Q. 25. In rust cycle the cereal host is infected by

Ans. Aeciospores

Q. 26. Tea rust is caused by

Ans. Algae

Q. 27. *Colletotrichum falcatum* produces

Ans. Conidospores

Q. 28. Citrus greening is caused by

Ans. *Fastedious bacteria*

Q.29 . Shape of MLO IS

Ans. Polymorphic

Q. 30. MLO disease is transmitted by

Ans. Leaf hopper

Q. 31. Rice blast pathogen perfect stage is

Ans. *Magnaporthe grisea/Pyricularia grisea*

Q. 32. Rice blast pathogen Imperfect stage is

Ans. *Pyricularia oryzae*

Q. 33. Sterlity disease of pigeonpea spread by

Ans. Mites

Q. 34. Powdery mildew includes in subdivision

Ans. Ascomycotina

Q. 35. Downy mildew includes in subdivision

Ans. Oomycetes

Q. 36. Soil microorganisms are most active at

Ans. 34-36^{0}C

Q. 37. Phylloidy disease of Seasame spread by

Ans. Leaf hopper

Q. 38. Nuclear Polyhedrosis Virus (NPV) is most effective for control of

Ans. Helicoverpa armigera

Q. 39. Vector of Little leaf of Brinjal is

Ans. Brown plant hopper

Q. 40. Most widely used fungicide for the control of Smut funfi is

Ans. Vitavax

Q. 41. Most widely used fungicide for the control of powdery mildew

Ans. Calaxin

Q. 42. Widely used fungicide for rust fungi is

Ans. Dithane M-45

Q. 43. Sexual, thick walled and resting spores of the rust fungi is known as

Ans. Teliospores

Q. 44. Mature particle of plant viruses is known as

Ans. Virion

Q. 45. Blast of rice is caused by (Rotten neck)

Ans. *Pyricularia oryzae*

Q. 46. Bacterial blight of rice is caused by (Kresek symptoms)

Ans. *Xanthomonas oryzae*

Q. 47. Bunt of rice is caused by

Ans. *Neovossia horrida*

Q. 48. Sheath rot of rice is caused by

Ans. *Rhizoctonia oryzae*

Q. 49. Reduced O_2 and N_2 under submerged conditions causes

Ans. Tip burn of Paddy

Q. 50. Brown leaf spot of rice is caused by

Ans. *Helminthosporium oryzae*

Q. 51. False smut of rice is caused by

Ans. *Ustilaginoidea virens/Claviceps oryzae*

Q. 52. Stem rot of Paddy is caused by

Ans. *Sclerotium oryzae*

Q. 53. Foot rot disease in rice is due to

Ans. *Gibberella fujikoral*

Q. 54. Grassy stunt virus of rice is transmitted by

Ans. Brown Plant Hopper

Q. 55. Leaf blight of wheat is caused by

Ans. *Alternaria triticina*

Q. 56. Loose smut of wheat is caused by

Ans. *Ustilago tritici*

Q. 57. Black or Stem rust of wheat is caused by

Ans. *Puccinia graminis*

Q. 58. Stripe rust or Yellow rust of wheat is caused by

Ans. *Puccinia striiformis/Puccinia glumaram*

Q. 59. Brown rust or Leaf rust of wheat is caused by

Ans. *Puccinia recondita*

Q. 60. Powder mildew of wheat is caused by

Ans. *Erysiphe graminis*

Q. 61. Flag smut of wheat is caused by

Ans. *Urocystis tritici*

Q. 62. Karnal bunt also known as Indian bunt of wheat is caused by

Ans. *Tilletia indica*

Q. 63. Hill bunt of wheat or stinking smut is due to

Ans. *Tilletia foetida/Tilletia tritici*

Q. 64. Black mould of wheat is due to

Ans. Cladosporium

Q. 65. Glume blotch of wheat is caused by

Ans. *Septoria nodorum*

Q. 66. Leaf blotch of wheat is caused by

Ans. *Septoria tritici*

Q. 67. Yellow ear rot ot yellow slime disease of wheat is caused by

Ans. *Clavibacter tritici*

Q. 68. Red stripe of sugarcane is caused due to

Ans. *Pseudomonas rubrilineans*

Q. 69. Red spot of sugarcane is caused due to

Ans. *Leptosphaeria sacchari*

Q. 70. Red rot of sugarcane is caused due to

Ans. *Colletotrichum falcatum*

Q. 71. Mosaic of sugarcane is caused due to

Ans. Sugarcane mosaic Virus

Q. 72. Fiji disease of sugarcane is caused due to

Ans. Fisi virus

Q. 73. Sereh disease of sugarcane which results in blackening and degeneration of the fanlike tops, is caused due to

Ans. Virus

Q. 74. Wilt disease of sugarcane is caused due to

Ans. *Cephalosporium sacchari*

Q. 75. Grassy spot of sugarcane is caused due to

Ans. MLO

Q. 76. Gumming disease of sugarcane is caused due to

Ans. *Xanthomonas campestris pv vascularum*

Q. 77. White rust of crucifers is caused due to

Ans. *Albugo candida*

Q. 78. Alternaria blight of crucifers is caused due to

Ans. *Alternaria brassicae*

Q. 79. Downy mildew of mustard is caused due to

Ans. *Peronospora brassicae*

Q. 80. Blight of mustard is caused due to

Ans. *Alternaria brassicae*

Q. 81. Black wart of potato is caused due to

Ans. *Synchytricum endobioticum*

Q. 82. Late blight of potato is caused due to

Ans. *Phytophthera infestans*

Q. 83. Early blight of potato is caused due to

Ans. *Alternaria solani*

Q. 84. Leaf roll of potato is caused due to

Ans. Potato leaf roll virus 'luteo virus'

Q. 85. Purple top of potato is caused due to

Ans. MLO

Q. 86 . Black heart of potato is caused due to

Ans. Unfavourable O_2 condition during storage

Q. 87. Ring disease of potato is caused due to

Ans. *Pseudomonas solanacearum*

Q. 88. Leaf roll of potato is caused due to

Ans. Solanum virus 14

Q. 89. Leaf spot of groundnut or tikka disease is caused due to

Ans. *Cercosporidium personatum* or *Cercospora arachidicola*

Q. 90. Collar rot of groundnut is caused due to

Ans. *Aspergillus niger*

Q. 91. Wilt of cotton is caused due to

Ans. *Fusarium oxysporium f. sp.vainfectum*

Q. 92. Black arm or bacterial blight of cotton is caused due to

Ans. *Xanthomonas malvacearum*

Q. 93. Leaf spot or leaf blight of cotton is caused due to

Ans. *Alternaria macrospora*

Q. 94. Fusarium wilt of cotton is caused due to

Ans. *Fusarium vasinfectum*

Q. 95. Root rot in cotton is caused due to

Ans. *Rhizocotonia bataticola*

Q. 96. Vericular Arbuscular Mycorrhizas (VAS) ia a

Ans. Fungi

Q. 97. Black eye rot is a disease of

Ans. Water chestnut

Selective Questions of Entomology

Q.1. Pheramone trap attracts

Ans. Male moths

Q. 2. Dimethoate is a

Ans. Systemic insecticide

Q. 3. Erisilkworm is released on

Ans. Castor

Q. 4. The worker bee is a

Ans. Sterile female

Q. 5. Stem injection or root feeding of monocrotophos is recommended for the management of

Ans. Coconut black headed caterpillar

Q. 6. Granular insecticide having long residual effect is

Ans. Aldicarb

Q. 7. Insecticide that belong to organophosphate group

Ans. Malathion

Q. 8. Project directorate of biological control is located at

Ans. Bangalore

Q. 9. Red cotton bug lay its egg on

Ans. Soil

Q. 10. Holes at the base of Sorghum peduncle are due to

Ans. *Chilo partellus*

Q. 11. Probosis in mouth parts of the butterfly is formed from

Ans. Galea of maxilla

Q. 12. Halfmoon shaped scarping or notching of the brinjal leaves are due to

Ans. *Myllocerus subfaciantus*

Q. 13. Aphids that causes bunch top of banana

Ans. *Pentalonia nigronervosa*

Q. 14. Mustard saw fly lays egg near

Ans. Leaf margin

Q. 15. Cotton leaf curl is caused by

Ans. Whit fly

Q. 16. Central Plant Protection Training Institute is located at

Ans. Hyderabad

Q. 17. NCIPM is located at

Ans. New Delhi

Q. 18. Central Insecticide Laboratory is located at

Ans. Faridabad

Q. 19. Sterile insect technique was first time proposed in the year 1937 by

Ans. Knipling

Q. 20. Biocontrol agent of Lantana weed is

Ans. *Ophiomyia lantanae*

Q. 21. *Bacillus thuringinensis* was discovered by

Ans. S. Ishiwata

Q. 22. An allelochemical beneficial to releaser only is called

Ans. Allomone

Q. 23. Kairomone is beneficial to

Ans. Receiver only

Q. 24. Synomone is beneficial to

Ans. Receiver and emitter only

Q. 25. Antimone are non-adventageous to

Ans. Both receiver and releaser

Q. 26. In honey bees, the queen substance is secreted by

Ans. Mandibular glands

Q. 27. Type of mouth parts present in honey bee is

Ans. Chewing and lapping type

Q. 28. Father of Insect physiology is

Ans. Wiggelworth

Q. 29. Term IPM was propounded by

Ans. Geiger & Clark (1961)

Q. 30. Insecticide act was passed in the year

Ans. 1968

Q. 31. Pest occurs in same area, year after year

Ans. Endemic pest

Q. 32. Pest occurs in area in severe form

Ans. Epidemic pest

Q. 33. Pest occurs in few isolated localities

Ans. Sporadic pest

Q. 34. Pest occurs most frequently on cultivated crops

Ans. Regular pest

Q. 35. Borers can be controlled biologically by

Ans. *Trichograma japonicum*

Q. 36. Rosetting of flowers is due to

Ans. *Pictinophora gossypiella (Pink bollworm)*

Q. 37. Vector of *Gossypium hirsutum* virus that causes leaf curl is

Ans. Whit fly

Q. 38. Vector of cotton leaf curl virus is

Ans. *Bemisia tabaci*

Q. 39. Scientific name of sugarcane shoot borer is

Ans. *Chilo infuscatellus*

Q. 40. Bunchy top appearance in sugarcane is due to

Ans. *Scirpophaga excerptaels*/Top borer

Q. 41. Name of the rice yellow stem borer which is a monophagus insect is

Ans. *Scirpophaga incertuls*

Q. 42. Hopper burn in cotton is due to

Ans. *Amrasca biguttula*

Q. 43. The crop having highest consumption of pesticide (54%) is

Ans. Cotton

Q. 44. The scientific name of BPH of rice is

Ans. *Nilaparvta lugens*

Q. 45. The viruses transmitted by Brown Plant Hopper are

Ans. Rice ragged stunt virus and Rice grassy stunt virus

Q. 46. Rice variety resistant to BPH IS

Ans. IR64

Q. 47. Insect that causes 100% crop loss in Paddy at high population density and hopper burn is

Ans. BPH

Q. 48. Serious pest of wheat are

Ans. White gurb and termite

Q. 49. Helicovepra and *Agrotis ipsilon* are the serious pest of

Ans. Chickpea

Q. 50. Serious pest of rice is

Ans. *Scirpophaga incertutas* (Yellow stem borer)

Selective Questions of Agriculture Extension

Q.1. Father of extension education is

Ans. James Stuart

Q. 2. Father of extension in India

Ans. K.N. Singh

Q. 3. First union minister for cooperation and panchyati raj is

Ans. S.K. Dey

Q. 4. Marginal farmers have land less than

Ans. 2.5 Acres

Q. 5. Small farmers have land less than

Ans. 5 Acres

Q. 6. Big farmers have land more than

Ans. 10 Acres

Q. 7. CDP started in

Ans. 2nd of Oct. 1952 (S.K. Dey)

Q. 8. NES started in

Ans. 2nd of Oct. 1953 (S.K Dey)

Q. 9. IADP started in

Ans. 1960-61

Q. 10. IAAP started in

Ans. 1964

Q. 11. Antyoda Yojna or movement started in

Ans. 2nd of Oct. 1977

Q. 12. TRYEM started on

Ans. August 1979

Q. 13. Jawahar Rozgar Yojna started in

Ans. 28th of April 1989

Q. 14. T&V Program evolved in 1973 by

Ans. D. Benor

Q. 15. T&V Program started in India in

Ans. 1974

Q. 16. IRDP started in

Ans. 2nd of Oct. 1980

Q. 17. Lab to Land program started in

Ans. 1979

Q. 18. Visual Aid Pictures are

Ans. Flash cards, Flannel graph

Q. 19. Audio Visual Aid Pictures are

Ans. Puppet, Cinema projector, Drama, Video, TV, LCD, LED, VCD

Q. 20. New agriculture strategy or Green revolution started in

Ans. 1966

Q. 21. HYVP (High yielding variety program) started in

Ans. 1966

Q. 22. Multiple cropping program started in

Ans. 1966

Q. 23. DLAD (Dry Land Area Development) started in

Ans. 1970

Q. 24. NCA (National Commission for Agriculture) started in

Ans. 1970

Q. 25. NREP (National Rural Employment Program) started in

Ans. 1977

Q. 26. Cooperative Credit Society Act passed on

Ans. 1904

Q. 27. Maharastra Zila parished & Panchayat Samiti Act was enacted in

Ans. 1961

Q. 28. Sequence of phases of Mental Process is

Ans. Awareness → Interest → Action → Satisfaction

Q. 29. Sequence of phases of communication process is

Ans. Communication → Channel → Message → Audience

Q. 30. Adopters sequence is

Ans. Innovators → Early adopters → Early majority → Late majority → Laggards

Q. 31. Goal of agriculture extension is

Ans. To promote income of farmers

Q. 32. First KVK established at

Ans. Pondichery in 1974

Q. 33. Fundamental objective of extension education is

Ans. The development of the people

Q. 34. First state to adopt T&V program is

Ans. Rajasthan

Q. 35. Word extension was first used in

Ans. 1873

Q. 36. Etawah Pilot Project

Ans. Albert Mayer (1948)

Q. 37. Gurgaon Project

Ans. F.L. Bryne (1920)

Q. 38. Sevagarm Project

Ans. M.K. Gandhi (1929)

Q. 39. Shriniketan attempt was started by R.N. Tagore in collaboration with Elmhirst in

Ans. West Bengal

Q. 40. Tagore and Agricultural economist Leonard Elmhirst set up the "Institute for Rural Reconstruction" in the year

Ans. 1921

Q. 41. Institute for Rural Reconstruction was later renamed as

Ans. Shriniketan or Adobe of welfare

Q. 42. Marathandum project

Ans. Spancer Hatch(1921)

Q. 43. Extension education originated from

Ans. Japan

Q. 44. Model Village given by

Ans. Daniel Hamilton (1903)

Q. 45. Firka development scheme given by

Ans. T. Prakashan (1946)

Q. 46. The best PRA exercise for farming system is

Ans. Resource mapping

Q. 47. The source of interview best in rural society

Ans. Focussed group

Q. 48. Role of different agencies for village development is included in

Ans. Chapati diagram

Q. 49. Grow more food campaign launched in

Ans. 1948

Q. 50. Grow more food campaign enquiry committee

Ans. 1952

Q. 51. Intensive cattle development program

Ans. 1964

Q. 52. Panchayti Raj first started in

Ans. 2nd of Oct. 1959 in Nagpur (Rajasthan)

Q. 53. Sequence of steps in extension teaching are

Ans. Attention → Interest → Desire → Conviction → Action → Satisfaction

Q. 54. The sequence of innovation decision process or adoption process is

Ans. Awareness → Interest → Evaluation → Trial → Adoption

Q. 55. Leaflet is a single sheet of paper folded to make how page pieces of printed matter?

Ans. 4

Q. 56. For one talk how many Flash cards should be used

Ans. 10-12

Q. 57. Extension is derived from

Ans. Latin word

Q. 58. A series of still pictures on one roll is called

Ans. Film stripes

Q. 59. A bulletin should contain how many pages?

Ans. 24-48 pages

Q. 60. Rural system research idea was motivated by M.S. Swaminathan in the year

Ans. 1988

Q. 61. Operational research projects were initiates in

Ans. 1970-71

Q. 62. Term community development originated from

Ans. Cambridge in England in 1946

Q. 63. "Communication process" in rural development is written by

Ans. Leagans

Q. 64. The expressions of the ends towards which our efforts are directed are called

Ans. Objectives

Q. 65. The distance in any direction one expects to go during a given period of time is called

Ans. Goal

Q. 66. Gap between the situation and objectives is the area of

Ans. Needs

Q. 67. Farm demonstration work begin in 1903 in USA by

Ans. Dr Seaman

Q. 68. Royal commission report came in

Ans. 1928

Q. 69. Self sufficiency in food grains was achieved in

Ans. 4th five year plan (1969-74)

Q. 70. Term Sociometery was coined by

Ans. Jacob Moreno

Q. 71. Those things which person ought or ought not to do in society are called

Ans. Moral

Q. 72. Adopters category which respect and regarded by many others in the social system as a role model are called

Ans. Early adopters

Q. 73. Young farmers association was farmed in India under the guidance of Dr. P.S. Deshmusk in the year

Ans. April' 1956

Q. 74. National commission on farmers was setup in India on

Ans. 10th of Feb' 2004

Q. 75. First chairman of National Commission on farmers

Ans. Sompal Singh Shastri (2004)

Q. 76. National food for work programme was launched in

Ans. Nov. 14th 2004

Q. 77. Swarnjayanti Gram Swarozgar Yojana (SGSY) was launched in

Ans. April, 1999

Q. 78. Firka development scheme launched under guidance of

Ans. T. Prakasam (1946)

Q. 79. National Agriculture Technology Project (NATP) started in

Ans. 1998-1999

Q. 80. The rate of extension worker in extension education is to create an effective

Ans. Learning situation

Q. 81. National demonstrations are the first line demonstrations conducted on the farmers field by

Ans. Research scientists

Q. 82. National demonstration started in India in the Year

Ans. 1956

Q. 83. Agriculture finance is the study of financing the farm business given by

Ans. Murray and Nelson

Q. 84. The incidence of debit per acre of land holding was highest in the state of

Ans. Bihar

Q. 85. The community development block passes through

Ans. Four stages of development

Q. 86. Basic unit of development under IRD programme is

Ans. A family

Q. 87. Basic operational unit for rural development in India is

Ans. Block

Q. 88. In India, the use of television as a medium of communication for rural development was started in the year

Ans. 1967

Q. 89. Rural development programmes should be formed to meet

Ans. Short term, emergent and long term changes

Q. 90. Gram sevika is responsible for village women education about

Ans. Rural development programme.

Q. 91. UNICEF was established in the year

Ans. 1946

Q. 92. UNESCO was established in the year

Ans. 1947

Q. 93. NABARD was established in the year

Ans. July, 1982

Q. 94. The price below which farmer is not ready to sell is known as

Ans. Reserve price

Q. 95. Food grain production include the production of

Ans. Cereals and Pulses

Q. 96. Total number of Krishi Vigyan Kendra (KVK) by March 2016

Ans. 645

Q. 97. Total number of Krishi Vigyan Kendra (KVK) in J&K

Ans. 19

Q. 98. Total number of Krishi Vigyan Kendra (KVK) in Punjab

Ans. 20

Q. 99. Total number of Krishi Vigyan Kendra (KVK) in Uttar Pradesh

Ans. 68

Q. 100. Out of the eight zones which one has the highest number of KVK's

Ans. Zone VII (100 in numbers)

Q. 101. Father of extension education in India is

Ans. K.N. Singh

Q. 102. Pradhanmantri Jal Samvardhan Yojana started in the year

Ans. 2002

Q. 103. Integrated Scheme of Oilseed, Pulses, Oil palm & maize (ISOPOM) was started in the year

Ans. 2004

Q. 104. Food security and quality year was declared on

Ans. 2008-2009

Q. 105. The committee that recommended ASRB is

Ans. Gajendra Gadkar Committee

Q. 106. First national conference of KVK was held in the year 2005 at

Ans. New Delhi

Q. 107. Weather based crop insurance scheme (WBCIS) started in the year

Ans. 2010

Q. 108. Father of PRA

Ans. Robert Chmabers

Q. 109. Integrated Child Protection Scheme started in the year

Ans. 2009

Q. 110. Village Grain Bank Scheme started in the year

Ans. 1996-97

Q. 111. National Rural Health Mission (NRHM) started in the year

Ans. 12th of April, 2005

Selective Questions of Plant Physiology

Q.1. Father of plant physiology

Ans. Stephen Hales

Q. 2. Father of Indian physiology

Ans. R.N. Dastur

Q. 3. Increasing order of respiratory quotient are

Ans. Fats (0.7)< Protiens (0.8-0.9)< Carbohydrates (1)< Malic Acid (1.33) < Oxalic acid (4)

Q. 4. Leghaemoglobin regulate oxygen in

Ans. Root nodules of plants

Q. 5. Photorespiration is high in

Ans. C_3 plants

Q. 6. Ribosomes are produced in

Ans. Nucleolus

Q. 7. Protein synthesis takes place in

Ans. Rough endoplasmic reticulum

Q. 8. Enzyme that convert ammonia to amino acid

Ans. Glutamine synthetase

Q. 9. Enzyme associated with decarboxylation reaction in photosynthetic reaction of C_4 plants is

Ans. Malic enzyme

Q. 10. Ultimate electron donor in mitochondrial e^- transport chain is

Ans. Ubiquinon

Q. 11. Precursor of ethylene biosynthesis is

Ans. Methionine

Q. 12. Chemical nature of GA_3 is

Ans. Terpene

Q. 13. Micronutrient essential for synthesis of auxin is

Ans. Zn

Q. 14. Hormone associated with acid growth theory is

Ans. Zn

Q. 15. Natural inhibitor of IAA oxidases is

Ans. Coumaric acid

Q. 16. Zeatin first isolated from corn seed by

Ans. D.S. Letham

Q. 17. Precursor of gibberellic acid is

Ans. Kaurene

Q. 18. Hormone which promote germination of dormant seeds and growth of dormant buds is

Ans. GA_3

Q. 19. During germination, embryo normally provides which hormone to the aleurone layer for the manufacturing of hydrolytic enzyme (á-amylase)

Ans. GA_3

Q. 20. Natural occurring cytokinins are

Ans. Zeatin and kinetin

Q. 21. Precursor of cytokinins is

Ans. Isopentenyl adenine

Q. 22. Precursor of ABA is

Ans. Violaxanthin

Q. 23. Aminoethoxyvinyl glycine (AVG) Inhibits

Ans. Ethylene biosynthesis

Q. 24. In rapidly transpiring plant the water column in xylem will be

Ans. -ve pressure

Q. 25. Site of oxidative electron transport in cell is

Ans. Mitochondria

Q. 26. Guttation is not favoured under

Ans. Low root pressure

Q. 27. Root pressure theory given by

Ans. Pristley (1916)

Q. 28. Relay pump theory was given by

Ans. Godlewski (1884)

Q.29. Pulsation theory was given by

Ans. J.C. Bose (1923)

Q. 30. Laminar theory or Sandwich theory (phosholipid bilayer) was given by

Ans. Daniel and Davson (1935)

Q. 31. Unit membrane theory (Trilaminar theory) was given by

Ans. Robertson (1959)

Q. 32. Fluid mosaic theory or Cell membrane theory was given by

Ans. Singer and Nicholson (1972)

Q. 33. Storage of elements in vacuoles occur under

Ans. Luxury consumption

Q. 34. Siderophores produced by fungi and bacteria in soil are the source of

Ans. Iron

Q. 35. The young leaves chlorotic, principal veins remain typically green, stalks slender and short are the deficiency symptoms of

Ans. Iron

Q. 36. Iron stored in chloroplast as an Iron protein complex is called

Ans. Phytoferritin

Q. 37. Water potential of chemically pure water is

Ans. Zero

Q. 38. Water potential of flaccid cell is

Ans. -10

Q. 39. Water potential of plasmolysed cell is

Ans. -12

Q. 40. Little leaf and rosette of apple and white bud of maize are the deficiency of

Ans. Zn

Q. 41. Under excessive light level synthesis of

Ans. Zeaxanthin increases

Q. 42. Mycorrhiza increased the availability of

Ans. Phosphorus

Q. 43. Vesicular arbuscular mycorrhiaze (VAM) is mostly used in

Ans. Perennial trees

Q. 44. Plastocyanin protein contains

Ans. Cu

Q. 45. Photons required to produce 1-molecule of oxygen are

Ans. 8

Q. 46. In C_3 plants, Rubisco enzyme first reacts with $CO-_2$ to form

Ans. PGA

Q. 47. Nitrate reductase is found in

Ans. Cytoplasm

Q. 48. In C_4 plants, the first stable product of photosynthesis is

Ans. Oxalic acid

Q. 49. Biological clock term coined by

Ans. Erwin Bunning

Q. 50. Photorespiration is alos known as

Ans. Glycolate pathway

Q. 51. Present level of CO_{2-} in atmosphere is

Ans. 360-370 ppm

Q. 52. In C_{4-} plants, enzyme responsible for the synthesis of Malic acid is

Ans. PEP carboxylase

Q. 53. The most striking feature of CAM plants is formation of

Ans. Malic acid at night

Q. 54. In C_3 plants, enzyme which reacts first with CO_2 to form PGA is

Ans. Rubisco

Q. 55. Transpiration ratio is highest in

Ans. C_3 plants

Q. 56. Electron transport takes place in which part of mitochondria

Ans. Cristae

Q. 57. Krebs cycle produces how many ATP's

Ans. 30

Q. 58. Negative phototropism growth or movement away from light is called

Ans. Skototropism

Q. 59. When the movement is towards the stimulus, it is called

Ans. Positive tropism

Q. 60. When the movement is away from the stimulus, it is called

Ans. Negative tropism

Q. 61. The movement in response to sunlight is called

Ans. Phototropism

Q. 62. The movement towards or away from the earth

Ans. Geotropism

Q. 63. The movement in which a plant moves or grows in response to touch or contact stimuli is called

Ans. Thigmotropism

Q. 64. The roots exhibits which type of geotropism

Ans. Positive geotropism

Q. 65. The stem exhibits which type of geotropism

Ans. Negative geotropism

Q. 66. Serine amino acid is produced in

Ans. Photorespiration

Q. 67. Aerenchyma is related with

Ans. Ethylene

Q. 68. Conversion of organic nitrogen to ammonium (NH_4^+) by soil microbes is called

Ans. Ammonification

Q. 69. Process by which N_2 is reduced to ammonium is called

Ans. Nitrogen fixation

Q. 70. Nitrogen fixation is carried out by enzyme nitrogenase which consists of

Ans. Fe-Mo-Protein

Q. 71. Law of limiting factor was given by

Ans. FF Blackman (1905)

Q. 72. The concept of 'law of minimum' was first given by

Ans. Liebig (1843)

Q. 73. Calvin cycle that are needed to produce one molecule of glucose are

Ans. Six

Q. 74. The movement of secondary branches of roots and stem growing at right angle is known as

Ans. Diageotropism

Q. 75. Seeds that are stimulated to germinate by light are described as

Ans. Positively photoblastic

Q. 76. Seeds whose germination is inhibited by light are said to be

Ans. Negatively photoblastic

Q. 77. The response of a seed to light is apparently mediated by a

Ans. Phytochrome

Q. 78. Positive photoblastic plants include

Ans. *Nicotiana tabacum*

Q. 79. The total amount of water present in soil is called

Ans. Holard

Q. 80. Copper deficiency in cereals, oats, beet and pulses causes

Ans. White tip disease

Q. 81. Primary acceptor of CO_2 fixation in CAM plant is

Ans. PEP

Q. 82. Primary acceptor of CO_2 fixation in C_3 plants is

Ans. RuBP

Q. 83. Highest water use efficiency in increasing order in plants

Ans. CAM> C_4> C_3

Q. 84. Calvin cycle (C_3 Cycle) and Hatch-Slack pathway (C_4 Cycle) occur in

Ans. Chloroplast

Q. 85. Photosynthetic ratio is highest in

Ans. C_4 plants

Q.86. First product of Photosynthesis is

Ans. 3PGA

Q. 87. Harvest index in cereals is

Ans. 0.4 to 0.5

Q. 88. Harvest index in pulses is

Ans. 0.2 to 0.3

Q. 89. Two processes that involve the mechanism of respiration are

Ans. Glycolysis and Kreb cycle

Q. 90. Exchange of gases in plants occurs through

Ans. Stomata and lenticles

Q. 91. Photophosphorilation occur in peroxisomes in association with

Ans. Chloroplast and mitochondria

Q. 92. Examples of C_4 plants are

Ans. Maize, Sugarcane, Sorghum

Q. 93. CAM pathway is found in plants such as

Ans. Pineapple, Agave, Opuntia, Cactus, Shishal

Q. 94. Photophosphorylation was discovered in chloroplasts by

Ans. D. Arnon

Q. 95. Dark reaction or light independent reaction or thermochemical reaction was given by

Ans. Calvin

Q. 96. Light reaction or photochemical reaction or Hill reaction occur in presence of

Ans. Ferric cyanide

Selective Questions of Genetics and Plant Breeding

Q.1. Seven characters studied by G.J. Mendel were located on

Ans. Four chromosomes

Q. 2. Sex form in most cucurbits including melons is

Ans. Monoecious

Q. 3. Test ratio in case of duplicate gene action will be

Ans. 3:1

Q. 4. Term gene was coined by

Ans. Johannsen

Q. 5. Concept of circular chromosomes in E. Coli was given by

Ans. Cairns

Q. 6. Cell linkage theory was proposed by

Ans. Virchow

Q. 7. DNA polymerase-I was discovered by

Ans. Kornberg

Q. 8. Stalk of the ovules is called

Ans. Funicle

Q. 9. Pusa gold is a new variety of

Ans. Wheat

Q. 10. Pusa Sugandha-5 is a new variety of

Ans. Rice

Q. 11. Pusa 1088, Pusa 1103, Pusa 1105 are new varieties of

Ans. Chickpea

Q. 12. Test ratio in case of complementary gene action will be

Ans. 1:3

Q. 13. Balanced tertiary trisomics (BTT) are associated with

Ans. Barley

Q. 14. The number of single crosses would be calculated by

Ans. n(n-1)/2

Q. 15. The number of double crosses would be calculated by

Ans. n(n-1) (n-2) (n-3) /8

Q. 16. The number of three way crosses would be calculated by

Ans. n(n-1) (n-2) /2

Q. 17. In cabbage cross pollination is due to

Ans. Self incompatibility

Q. 18. In Maize cross pollination is due to

Ans. Protoandry

Q. 19. The smallest unit of genetic material that cannot be divided but is interchangeable among units refers to

Ans. Recon

Q. 20. In apomixes progeny closely resembles

Ans. Female parent

Q. 21. Inbred lines in maize are maintained by

Ans. Self pollination

Q. 22. First cotton hybrid variety in the world developed in India

Ans. H4

Q. 23. Bulbosum technique is used in barley for production of

Ans. Haploids

Q. 24. Translocation involves

Ans. Non-homologous chromosomes

Q. 25. Coupling and repulsion hypothesis was given by

Ans. Bateson

Q. 26. DNA can be denatured by heating at a temperature of

Ans. 94^0C

Q. 27. Oxysomes occur in

Ans. Mitochondria

Q. 28. Genetically most pure seed is

Ans. Nucleus seed

Q.29. Maize is Monoecious and cross pollinated due to

Ans. Protoandry

Q. 30. Pearlmillet is

Ans. Protogyny

Q. 31. The male genetic nuclei are the results of mitotic division from

Ans. Generative nucleus

Q. 32. In primary trisomic, the extra chromosome is

Ans. Normal one

Q. 33. Brittle-2 is the mutant source of high lysine in

Ans. Maize

Q. 34. In nuts and oil seeds the limiting amino acid is

Ans. Lysine

Q. 35. In cereals limiting amino acid is

Ans. Lysine, threonine and sometimes tryptophan

Q. 36. In pulses limiting amino acid is

Ans. Methionine and tryptophan

Q. 37. In green vegetables limiting amino acid is

Ans. Methionine

Q. 38. Hiproly is a high lysine mutant variety of

Ans. Barley

Q. 39. Naphal is a high lysine and protein variety of

Ans. Wheat

Q. 40. Atlas-66 is a high protein source variety of

Ans. Wheat

Q. 41. Deletion leads to alteration in

Ans. Gene number

Q. 42. Duplication was first observed by

Ans. C.B Bridges (1919)

Q. 43. Pseudo-dominance is associated with

Ans. Deletion

Q. 44. Translocation homozygotes lead to alteration in

Ans. Linkage map

Q. 45. Concept of plant type was introduced by

Ans. Jennings (1964)

Q. 46. The term ideotype was coined by

Ans. Donald (1968)

Q. 47. Concept of crop ideotype was developed in

Ans. Wheat

Q. 48. Rice ideotype was given by

Ans. Jennings (1964)

Q. 49. Wheat ideotype was given by

Ans. Donald (1968)

Q. 50. Barley ideotype was given by

Ans. Rasmusson (1987)

Q. 51. Maize ideotype was given by

Ans. Mock and Pearce (1975)

Q. 52. Ability of plants to maintain a favourable internal water balance under moisture stress is known as

Ans. Drought avoidance

Q. 53. Ability of plants to withstand low tissue water content is called

Ans. Drought tolerance

Q. 54. Ability of plants to grow, develop and reproduce under moisture deficit conditions is termed as

Ans. Drought resistance

Q. 55. Feature of the host plant which makes the host unfavourable or unattractive to insect for food, shelter or reproduction, a mechanism of insect resistance also called

Ans. Antixenosis/Non-preference/Non acceptance

Q. 56. Adverse effects of the host on feeding, development and reproduction of Insects pests is due to

Ans. Antibiosis

Q. 57. Basic requirement under protection of plant variety and farmers act (PPV & FA) is

Ans. Novelty, distinctiveness, uniformity and stability

Q. 58. As per the seed act 2004 the variety of field crops can be registered for

Ans. 15 years

Q. 59. As per the seed act 2004 the variety of perrenial crops can be registered for

Ans. 18 years

Q. 60. The Indian seed act 2004 replaces the seed Act of

Ans. 1966

Q. 61. All released and notified varieties which have not been protected are called

Ans. Extant varieties

Q. 62. A variety which has to be protected are called

Ans. Candidate variety

Q. 63. A variety derived from the initial variety and having most of the characters of the initial variety but clearly distinguishable from initial variety are called

Ans. Essentially derived variety

Q. 64. Chromosome line up at the equator of spindle in

Ans. Metaphase

Q. 65. Chromatids of chromosome move apart in

Ans. Anaphase

Q. 66. During cell division, spindle fibres join the

Ans. Kinetochore

Q. 67. A cell in mitotic prophase can be distinguished from a cell in meiotic prophase by formation of

Ans. Tetrads in a meiotic cell

Q. 68. Synaptonemal comples appears during

Ans. Meiosis-I

Q. 69. In meiosis, the chromatids separate during

Ans. Anaphase-II

Q. 70. Segregation of Mendelian factors occurs during

Ans. Anaphase-I

Q. 71. Synapsis/bivalent formation takes place in meiosis in

Ans. Zygotene

Q. 72. Termination occur during

Ans. Diakinesis

Q. 73. Meiosis was coined by

Ans. Frame and Moore

Q. 74. Mitosis was coined by

Ans. Flemming

Q. 75. Meiosis-II bring about separation of

Ans. Chrmatids

Q. 76. Chiasmata are first observed in

Ans. Diplotene

Q. 77. In mitosis nuclear envelop and nucleolus disappear during

Ans. Prophase

Q. 78. Sequence of phases in cell cycle is

Ans. $G_1 - S - G_2 - M$

Q. 79. Chiasma represents the site of

Ans. Crossing over

Q. 80. The term genetics, allele, homozygous, heterozygous, F_1 and F_2 were coined by

Ans. William Bateson

Q. 81. Two independent pair of gene which together produce the same trait, but alone these dominant gene don't show its effect are called

Ans. Complementary gene having ratio of 9:7

Q. 82. Two independent pair of gene which together produce a new trait, but alone these dominant gene show its own effects are called

Ans. Supplementary gene (9:3:3:1)

Q. 83. The presence of a dominant gene inhibits the expression of other dominant and recessive genes are called

Ans. Dominant epistasis or simple epistasis (having ration of 12:3:1)

Q. 84. The presence of a recessive homozygous gene at one locus (aa) inhibits the expression of non-allelic gene at other locus (BB, Bb), the later can produce their effect when dominant allel (AA, Aa) occur at first locus are called

Ans. Recessive epistasis (having ratio of 9:3:4)

Q. 85. Dominant allel at one locus and homozygous recessive allel at another locus produces the same effect are called

Ans. Dominant recessive epistasis or Inhibitory gene action (having ratio of 13:3)

Q.86 . Two or more independent genes present on different chromosome produces nearly the same phenotype and their effect is not cumulative are called

Ans. Duplicate gene action or duplicate dominant epistasis (having ratio of 15:1)

Q. 87. Two independent gene alone produces the same phenotype trait but when present together they show a double cumulative effect are called

Ans. Duplicate gene with cumulative effect (having ratio of 9:6:1)

Q. 88. Characters which are controlled by sex linked genes are known as

Ans. Sex linked characters

Q. 89. The genes which are present in the autosomes but the intensity of their expression depends upon the sex hormones are called

Ans. Sex influenced characters

Q. 90. Certain genes which produce characters in one sex only, but not in both the sexes are called

Ans. Sex limited characters

Q. 91. Characters which is governed by many genes and each gene has small, cumulative effect are called as

Ans. Quantitative characters

Q. 92. Characters which are governed by one or few genes and each gene has large individual effect are called as

Ans. Qualitative characters

Q. 93. The term cell membrane was given by

Ans. Nageli and Cramer (1855)

Q. 94. The term plasmalemma was given by

Ans. Plowe (1931)

Q. 95. Lamellar theory or Sandwich model was given by

Ans. Danielli and Davson (1935)

Q. 96. Unit membrane hypothesis was given by

Ans. Robertson (1959)

Q. 97. Fluid mosaic model was given by

Ans. Singer and Nicolson (1972)

Q. 98. Cell wall first observed by

Ans. Robert Hooke (1665)

Q. 99. The substance between the nucleus and plasma membrane containing various organelles and inclusion is called

Ans. Cytoplasm

Q. 100. Endoplasmic reticulum (ER) was first observed by

Ans. Porter (1945)

Q. 101. Ribosomes were discovered in 1953 and named as ribosomes by

Ans. George Palade in 1955

Q. 102. Golgi complex was discovered by

Ans. Camillo Golgi in 1898

Q. 103. Lysosomes were first reported by

Ans. Christain de Duve in 1955

Q. 104. The term Lysosomes were coined by

Ans. Novikoff

Q. 105. Mitochondria first seen by

Ans. Kolliker in 1880

Q. 106. Term mitochondria was named by

Ans. Benda in 1898

Q. 107. The term plastid was coined by

Ans. E. Haeckel in 1866

Q. 108. Chroloplasts were first seen by

Ans. Anton van Leeuwenhoek

Q. 109. Nucleus was first observed by

Ans. Anton van Leeuwenhoek

Q. 110. Nucleus was first described by

Ans. Robert brown in 1831

Q. 111. Term enzyme was coined by

Ans. Kuhne in 1878

Q. 112. Germplasm theory was proposed by

Ans. Weisman

Q. 113. DNA synthesis takes place in

Ans. S Phase

Q. 114. DNA polymerase I was discovered by

Ans. Kornberg

Q. 115. DNA as the genetic element was shown by the experiment of

Ans. Avery, MacLeod and McCarty

Q. 116. The pure line theory was proposed by

Ans. Johannsen in 1903

Q. 117. The phenomenon of linkage was first observed by

Ans. Bateson and Punnett in 1904

Q. 118. The one gene one enzyme hypothesis was proposed by

Ans. George Beadle and Edward Tatum in 1941

Q. 119. The operon concept of gene regulation was proposed by

Ans. F. Jacob and J. Monod in 1961

Q. 120. Chromosome theory of linkage was proposed by

Ans. Morgan and Castle in 1911

Q. 121. First eukaryotic genome to be sequenced in 1966 is of

Ans. *Saccharomyces cerevisiae* having size of 12Mbp

Q. 122. First genome of cellular organism to be sequenced in 1995 is of

Ans. *Haemophilus influenza* having sixe of 1.8Mbp

Q. 123. First genome sequenced in 1977 is of

Ans. Phi X 174 having size of 5.38Kb

Q. 124. First plasmid sequenced in 1979 is of

Ans. Plasmid pBR 322 having size of 4.3Kb

Q. 125. First crop to be sequenced in 2002 is of

Ans. Rice having size of 430Mbp

Q. 126. First plant to be sequenced in 2000 is of

Ans. *Arabidopsis thaliana* having size of 135Mbp

Q. 127. Microsatellite comprises three percent of human genome with an average density of one SSR per

Ans. 2Kb of sequences

Q. 128. Term homeostasis was coined by

Ans. Lerner in 1954

Q. 129. National biodiversity is located at

Ans. Chennai

Q. 130. Development of embryo directly from diploid cells of either nucellus or integument is known as

Ans. Adventive embryony

Q. 131. Development of embryo from the diploid egg cell of another embrosac developed from diploid tissue of archesproium, nucellus or integuments is called

Ans. Apospory

Q. 132. A cross between an inbred line and open pollinated variety is known as

Ans. Top cross or Inbred-variety cross

Q. 133. A cross between a single cross and open pollinated variety is known as

Ans. Double top cross

Q. 134. A hybrid progeny from a cross between two inbreds or purelines or varieties are

Ans. Single cross

Selective Questions of Soil Science

Q.1. Weight or mass per unit volume of a substance is known as

Ans. Density

Q. 2. Mass or weight of unit volume of soil solids only is known as

Ans. Particle density or true density

Q. 3. Mass or weight of unit volume of oven dry soil is known as

Ans. Bulk density or apparent density

Q. 4. Particle density varies from

Ans. 2.60 to 2.75g/cm^3

Q. 5. Bulk density varies from

Ans. 1.4 to 1.8 g/cm^3

Q. 6. Micropores which are usually filled with water and have a size of

Ans. Less than 0.06mm or 30μm

Q. 7. Macropores which are usually filled with air and are also known as non-capillary pores have a size of

Ans. More than 0.06mm

Q. 8. Origin of soil, its classification and description is known as

Ans. Pedology

Q. 9. The science which deals with weathering of rocks and mineral factors, processing of soil formation and classification of soils in recognised system is known as

Ans. Pedology

Q. 10. The scientific study of the relationship between soils and living things, including man's use of land is known as

Ans. Edaphology

Q. 11. The study of soil as natural habitat for plant is also known as

Ans. Edaphology

Q. 12. Water held with a force of 0.33 or 1/3 atmospheric pressure is called

Ans. Field capacity

Q. 13. Water in the micropores which is held at a tension ranging between field capacity to 31 atmosphere pressure is known as

Ans. Capillary water

Q. 14. Water which is held on the surface of colloidal particles by the dipole orientation between 31 to 10,000 atmosphere pressure and is unavailable to plants is known as

Ans. Hygroscopic water

Q. 15. Water held at negative tension of 1/3 atmospheric pressure or below 1/3 atmospheric pressure is known as

Ans. Gravitational water

Q. 16. The percentage of water held by soil at 15 atmospheric pressure is called

Ans. Wilting point

Q. 17. The water which lies between wilting coefficient (1/3 atmospheric pressure) and field capacity is known as

Ans. Available water

Q. 18. Arrangement of soil particles and their aggregates are known as

Ans. Soil structure

Q. 19. Relative proportion of various soil separates in a soil material is known as

Ans. Soil texture

Q. 20. Vertical proportion of the soil showing various layers from the surface to the parent material is called as

Ans. Soil profile

Q. 21. The unconsolidated mantle of weathered rock and soil material on the earth surface, loose earth material above the solid rock is called

Ans. Regolith

Q. 22. Highly salt tolerant crops are

Ans. Barley, Sugarbeet and Cotton

Q. 23. Acid tolerant crop is

Ans. Rice

Q. 24. The highest potential microbial activity and the highest potential rate of organic waste mineralization occurs in soils that are

Ans. Warm, moist and well aerated

Q. 25. The availability of Sulphur is not affected by

Ans. Soil reaction

Q. 26. Loss of nitrogen as gaseous ammonia (NH_3 in alkaline soils is known as

Ans. Volatilization

Q. 27. Conversion of nitrate into gaseous nitrogen or nitrous oxides is known as

Ans. De-nitrification

Q. 28. Change of organic nitrogenous compounds into ammonia in presence of enzyme nitrogenise is known as,

Ans. Ammonification

Q.29 . Fastest nitrogen fixing plant is

Ans. *Sesbania rostrata* (fixes150-180Kg N/Hac)

Q. 30. Most outstanding green manuring crop is

Ans. Sunhemp (*Crotolaria juncea)*

Q. 31. Soil is described as stomach of plant by

Ans. Aristotle

Q. 32. Term functional nutrients or metabolic nutrients was given by

Ans. D.J. Nicholas (1961)

Q. 33. Essential elements or essentiality of nutrients was proposed by

Ans. Arnon and Stout (1939)

Q. 34. Energy currency of plant is

Ans. Phosphorous

Q. 35. Energy storage elements are

Ans. C, N, P, and S

Q. 36. Energy exchange elements are

Ans. Hydrogen and Oxygen

Q. 37. World largest potash deposits are in

Ans. Saskatchewan (In Canada)

Q. 38. Country having monopoly in phosphorous deposits is

Ans. Morocco

Q. 39. Yellow rust in wheat is one the first foliar disease reported to be suppressed by

Ans. Chlorine

Q. 40. Principal nourishment of plant was water given by

Ans. Francis Bacon

Q. 41. Water was the sole nutrient of plants given by

Ans. J.B. Helmont

Q. 42. The law of minimum was given by

Ans. Liebig in 1862

Q. 43. For nitrification the optimum pH is

Ans. 7.5

Q. 44. Element that is metal component of urease enzyme is

Ans. Nickel

Q. 45. Intracellular deposits of silicon is known as

Ans. Plant opals

Q. 46. Microorganism which is a free fixer or in association with grasses is

Ans. Azospirillum

Q. 47. Diagnostic surface horizons are called

Ans. Epipedons

Q. 48. Specific heat of Humus is more than

Ans. Clay, silt an sand

Q. 49. Average content of silica in soil is

Ans. 27%

Q. 50. Taurmaline is crystalline

Ans. Boron-silicate mineral

Q. 51. Plasticity of soil is determined by

Ans. Atterberg's apparatus

Q. 52. Soil aggregation can be estimated by

Ans. Yoder's apparatus

Q. 53. Readily available form of 'K' in soil ranges from

Ans. 0.1-2.0%

Q. 54. Sulphur soil testing is determined by

Ans. $CaCl_2$

Q. 55. Grass tetany is caused in forage crops due to deficiency of

Ans. Mg

Q. 56. Neutral chelate is

Ans. Citric acid

Q. 57. Method adopted for testing of Zn, Fe, Cu, and Mn is

Ans. DTPA

Q. 58. The DTPA soil testing was originally developed by

Ans. Lindsay and Norvell

Q. 59. Aluminium toxicity is probably a limiting factor in acid soils, particularly when

Ans. pH<5.0 to 5.5

Q. 60. Dominant structure in grasslands is

Ans. Spheroidal

Q. 61. Total incoming solar radiation that is sbsorbed by the soil and can be used to warm it is

Ans. 10%

Q. 62. Microorganism which have highest biomass in soil is

Ans. Fungi

Q. 63. Indicator plant of 'Cu' is

Ans. Wheat

Q. 64. *Aspergillus niger* is used to test the status of

Ans. 'K' in the soil

Q. 65. Cabbage and Cauliflower are indicator plant of

Ans. N and Ca

Q. 66. Maize is indicator plant of

Ans. Zn

Q. 67. Sunflower is indicator plant of

Ans. Boron

Q. 68. Sugarbeet is an indicator plant of

Ans. Sodium

Q. 69. Wheat is an indicator plant of

Ans. Copper

Q. 70. Potato is an indicator plant of

Ans. Potassium

Q. 71. A soil profile having two sola, one above the other is known as

Ans. Bisequem profile

Q. 72. Law of restitution was proposed by

Ans. Liebig

Q. 73. Total number of master horizons present in soils are

Ans. Five

Q. 74. DTPA tests was developed by Linsday for extraction of

Ans. Micronutrient

Q. 75. Father of soil testing is

Ans. Troug

Q. 76. Fertility gradient approach was given by

Ans. B. Ramamoorthy

Q. 77. Hartig nets in soil produced by

Ans. Ectomycorrhiza

Q. 78. An ectomycorrhiza is a form of symbiotic relationship that occurs between a fungal symbiont and the

Ans. Roots of various plant species

Q. 79. Acidic soils are deficient in

Ans. Ca, Mg and P

Q. 80. Fulvic acid is soluble in both

Ans. Acid and alkali

Q. 81. Total numbers of 'ecological zones' of India are

Ans. 20

Q. 82. Agro-climatic zones of India are

Ans. 15

Q. 83. Kankar nodules are found mostly in

Ans. Red soils

Q. 84. Process of moving out of sesquioxide is known as

Ans. Podzolization

Q. 85. O-Horizon is absent in

Ans. Arable soils

Q.86 . Mechanical analysis of soils separation is done by

Ans. Hydrometric method

Q. 87. Soils which are most suitable for most of the crops are

Ans. Sandy loams

Q. 88. Bulk density of general soils is

Ans. 1.33 gm/cm^3

Q. 89. Total pore space is highest in

Ans. Clay soils

Q. 90. Humic acid is soluble in

Ans. Alkali

Q. 91. Fumic acid is soluble in

Ans. Both acid and alkali

Q. 92. Wood is mainly decomposed by

Ans. Actinomycetes

Q. 93. Organic matter content in Indian soils is generally

Ans. < 0.5%

Q. 94. Soil structure which is best for cultivation is

Ans. Crumby structure

Q. 95. Crops which absorbs ammonical form (NH_4^+) directly

Ans. Potato and Paddy

Q. 96. Indian soils are deficient in

Ans. Zn

Q. 97. Azotobacter and Beijernckia are

Ans. Aerobic bacteria

Q. 98. Azotobacter is used in crops such as

Ans. Rice, Cotton and sugarcane

Q. 99. Azospirillum is used in crops such as

Ans. Paddy, Jowar, wheat, maize, cotton, sugarcane

Q. 100. Application of clay to sandy soils is known as

Ans. Marling

Q. 101. Ammonical fertilizers should be applied in

Ans. Reduced zones

Q. 102. Nitrate fertilizers should be applied in

Ans. Oxidised zones

Q. 103. High lime requirement crops are

Ans. Sugarbeet and Soyabean

Q. 104. High salt tolerant crops are

Ans. Sugarbeet and barley

Q. 105. Acid tolerant crop is

Ans. Rice

Q. 106. Soils with pH<4 are known as

Ans. Cat soils

Q. 107. Electrical conductivity is used to express

Ans. Salinity of the soils

Q. 108. Microorganism having highest biomass in soil is

Ans. Fungi

Q. 109. Father of soil testing is

Ans. Emil Troug

Q. 110. Father of Pedology is

Ans. Vasily V Dokuchaev

Q. 111. Father of soil science is

Ans. Vasily V Dokuchaev

Q. 112. Father of agricultural chemistry

Ans. Justin Von Liebig

Q. 113. Fertilizer prices committee was constituted in

Ans. Jan' 1976

Q. 114. As per Operational Guidelines of Soil Health Card Scheme, samples to be collected and tested for irrigated area should be from a grid of

Ans. 2.5 Hectares

Q. 115. As per Operational Guidelines of Soil Health Card Scheme, samples to be collected and tested for rainfed area should be from a grid of

Ans. 10 Hectares

Q. 116. Nitrogen is absorbed by plant in the form of

Ans. Nitrate ($NO_3^{É}$) and ammonium (NH_4^+) form

Q. 117. Phosphorous is absorbed by plant in the form of

Ans. $H_2PO_4^{É}$ (Dihydrogen phosphate ion) and $HPO_4^{2É}$ (Hydroxyphosphate ion)

Q. 118. Boron is absorbed by plants in the form of

Ans. $B_4O_7^{2É}$ (Borate ion) and $H_2BO_3^{É}$ (Borate ion)

Selective Questions of Agronomy

Q.1. India has largest area in rice cultivation in world which is about

Ans. 45Mha

Q. 2. Sowing time of Boro or Dalua rice is

Ans. Dec-Jan

Q. 3. Sowing time for Aus/Autum/Kharif rice is

Ans. May-June

Q. 4. Sowing time for Aman/Winter rice is

Ans. June-July

Q. 5. In wet bed method of rice, seedlings are ready for transplantation in

Ans. 20-25 days

Q. 6. Tungro virus of rice is transmitted by

Ans. Green leaf hopper

Q. 7. Grassy stunt virus disease of rice is transmitted by

Ans. Brown plant hopper

Q. 8. Gundhi bug insect attack on rice during

Ans. Milking stage

Q. 9. Teat weight of basmati rice is

Ans. 21gm

Q. 10. The "Kresek" occur in early stage of plant growth of rice in

Ans. BLB

Q. 11. The soil carried in saltation consists of

Ans. 0.1 to 0.5mm particle size

Q. 12. The soil carried in suspension consists of

Ans. <0.1mm particle size

Q. 13. The soil carried in surface creep consists of

Ans. 5-10 mm particle size

Q. 14. Dead heart & white head damage to rice is caused by

Ans. Stem borer

Q. 15. Groundnut rostee disease due to virus is spread by

Ans. Aphid

Q. 16. Father of modern Agronomy is

Ans. Peter De-crescenzi

Q. 17. Phylloidy disease of seasamum spread by

Ans. Leaf hopper

Q. 18. Sterility mosaic disease of pigeon pea spread by

Ans. Mites

Q. 19. Yellow vein mosaic of Okra spread by

Ans. *Bemisia tabaci*

Q. 20. Yellow mosaic virus of mung caused by

Ans. *Aphis crassivora*

Q. 21. Leaf curl of tomato is caused by

Ans. White fly

Q. 22. Bunchy top of Papaya is spread by

Ans. Leaf hoppers

Q. 23. Best suited temperature for sugarcane growth is

Ans. 26-32°C

Q. 24. Adsali sugarcane is planted in

Ans. July-August

Q. 25. Element essential for sugar translocation in sugarcane is

Ans. K

Q. 26. Critical stage of Sugarcane is

Ans. Formative stage

Q. 27. Setts needed to plant 1-Hec. of sugarcane are

Ans. 35,000-40,000 setts

Q. 28. Epricania melanoleuca is a paraitoid effective against

Ans. Sugarcane pyrilla

Q.29. Congress grass (*Parthenium hysterophorous)*can be contolled by

Ans. *Zygogramma bocolarata*

Q. 30. The seed rate of hybrid maize is

Ans. 20-25 Kg/Hac

Q. 31. Sunflower is an indicator plant of

Ans. Boron

Q. 32. Optimum plant population of cotton/Hac is between

Ans. 50000-80,000 plants

Q. 33. Stevenson screen is related to

Ans. Agrometeorology

Q. 34. Botanical name of "Sewan grass" is

Ans. *Lasiurus sindicus*

Q. 35. Phytohormone involved in nutrient mobilization is

Ans. Auxin

Q. 36. At field capacity the value of pF is

Ans. 2.5

Q. 37. At permanent wilting point the value of pF is

Ans. 4.2

Q. 38. At saturation the value of pF is

Ans. 0

Q. 39. Stem nodulation occurs in green manure crop of

Ans. *Aeschynomene afraspera*

Q. 40. A-value concept was given by

Ans. Fried and Dean

Q. 41. Irrigation in gram are recommended at

Ans. Before flowering and pod formation stages

Q. 42. Aruna is a mutant variety of

Ans. Castor

Q. 43. Black cotton soil is rich in

Ans. Montmorillonite

Q. 44. Excess uptake of "K" element is known as

Ans. Luxury consumption

Q. 45. Test weight of Basmati rice is

Ans. 21 gm

Q. 46. Test weight of Wheat is

Ans. 40 gm

Q. 47. Test weight of mungbean is

Ans. 34-36 gm

Q. 48. Test weight of Sunflower is

Ans. 60-62 gm

Q. 49. Test weight of Pearl millet is

Ans. 5-7 gm

Q. 50. Test weight of Sorghum is

Ans. 25-30 gm

Q. 51. Ideal temperature for tuberization of potato is

Ans. 18^0C

Q. 52. In tobacco, chronological order of practices are

Ans. Topping-desuckering-priming

Q. 53. In India, first dry farming research station, Manjri was started in the year

Ans. 1923

Q. 54. Berseem introduced in India from Egypt in the year

Ans. 1904

Q. 55. Plants nutrient elements reaches roots by the process of diffusion is

Ans. P

Q. 56. Clay mineral found most in agriculture soils is

Ans. Phyllosilicates

Q. 57. P & K ions move from soil to roots of field crop by the process of

Ans. Diffusion

Q. 58. High organic matter content in soil reduces the availability of

Ans. Cu

Q. 59. Long term persistent herbicide is

Ans. Glyphostae

Q. 60. Pop pod in groundnut is due to deficiency of

Ans. Ca

Q. 61. Leaf colour chart is used for judging the amount of nitrogen in standing crop of

Ans. Rice

Q. 62. *Gossypium hirsutum* is predominant spp. of cotton grown in

Ans. India

Q. 63. AGMARK act was enforced in the year

Ans. 1937

Q. 64. Whole business of wheat in India was nationalised in the year

Ans. 1973

Q. 65. Cropping Intensity will be always 100 percent in

Ans. Monocropping

Q. 66. Trade name of butachlor is

Ans. Machete

Q. 67. Trade name of alachlor is

Ans. Lasso

Q. 68. Trade name of fluchoralin is

Ans. Basalin

Q. 69. Trade name of pendimethalin is

Ans. Stomp

Q. 70. Trade name of propanil is

Ans. Stam F-34

Q. 71. Trade name of trifluralin

Ans. Teflan

Q. 72. Striga is also known as

Ans. Witch weed

Q. 73. Host crops of striga are

Ans. Tobbaco, millets, maize, sugarcane, sunflower, sorghum

Q. 74. Host crops of orobanche are

Ans. Tomato, tobacco, carrot, sunflower, mustard, chilli, brinjal, potato

Q. 75. Cuscuta is associated with

Ans. Lucern, Alfalfa (*Medicago sativa*)

Q. 76. Cuscuta is also known as

Ans. Dodder

Q. 77. Striga is a semi-root parasite

Ans. Sorghum, maize etc

Q. 78. Orobanache is a total root parasite of

Ans. Tobacco, brinjal, tomato etc

Q. 79. Dodder which is also known as cuscuta is a

Ans. Total stem parasite

Q. 80. Loranthus which is also known as bird vine is a

Ans. Semi-stem parasite of mango, citrus, teak etc

Q. 81. The process of growing subsidiary crops between two widely spaced rows of main crop is known as

Ans. Inter cropping

Q. 82. When two or more crops are grown in succession with in a year is known as

Ans. Multiple cropping

Q. 83. The seeds of new crops are broadcasted before harvesting of standing crop is known as

Ans. Relay cropping

Q. 84. The process of growing two or more crops together in the same piece of land is known as

Ans. Mixed cropping

Q. 85. Process of growing different crops in succession on a piece of land in a specific period of time is known as

Ans. Crop rotation

Q.86 . The total yield of two crops is more than either of the main crop without creating any competition is known as

Ans. Synergetic crop

Q. 87. The system in which forests are managed for the production of wood as well as for rearing of domestic animals is known as

Ans. Silvi-pastoral system

Q. 88. When the land is managed for the concurrent production of agriculture and forest crops and for rearing of domestic animals is known as

Ans. Agri-silvi pastoral system

Q. 89. The conscious and deliberate use of land for the concurrent production of agriculture crops and forest crops is known as

Ans. Agri-silvi culture

Q. 90. Practice of forestry for the society, by the society, through the society, especially for fuel, fodder, fruits and small timber requirements is known as

Ans. Social forestry

Q. 91. Planting of trees on the sides of roads, canals and railways, along with planting on wasteland is known as

Ans. Extension forestry

Q. 92. The belt of trees/shrubs maintained for the purpose of shelters from wind, sun, snow-drift is known as

Ans. Shelter belts

Q. 93. *Trichogramma australicum* and *Trichogramma japonicum* controls

Ans. Sugarcane pest

Q. 94. *Trichogramma japonicum* and *Trichogramma brasiliensis* controls

Ans. St. Jose Scale of apple

Q. 95. *Platygaster oryzae* controls

Ans. Rice gall midge

Q. 96. Cocinella spp. controls

Ans. Aphids, whiteflies, scales, mealybuys

Q. 97. Cantharis spp. controls

Ans. Mealybugs and aphids

Q. 98. Rubber fly controls

Ans. Grasshopper, wasps, dragon flies

Q. 99. Tiger bettle controls

Ans. Variety of Insects

Q. 100. Dapog method of raising nursery of rice, has been introduced in India from

Ans. Philippines